The Short Stories of Manjeri Isvaran

A Study in Themes and Techniques

In the same series

M.V. Rama Sarma: His Mind and Art
K. Venkata Reddy, ed.

Studies in Indian Writing in English
P. Bayapa Reddy

Comparative Perspectives on Indian Literature
A. Ramakrishna Rao, ed.

Indian Literature Today (2 vols.)
R.K. Dhawan, ed.

Recent Indian Fiction
R.S. Pathak, ed.

Fiction of the Nineties
R.K. Dhawan and Veena Noble Dass, ed.

The Short Stories of Manjeri Isvaran

A Study in Themes and Techniques

N. Gopalakrishnan Nair

PRESTIGE

Published by
Prestige Books
New Delhi 110 008

ISBN: 81-7551-005-6

1996

Reprinted 2000

Photo Typesetting by
Pivot Computers
Delhi 110 006

Printed at
Mehra Offset Press
New Delhi 110 002

Contents

Contents

Preface

Manjeri S. Isvaran has been regarded, by common consent, a significant writer on the Indian literary scene. Although his contribution to Indian literature in English is substantial, with ten collections of poems, seventy-odd published short stories, two playlets, a book of criticism, a wide corpus of book reviews and essays and several unpublished works, it is as a writer of short stories that he is likely to be remembered by posterity because of the continuing popularity of the form and also because of his deftness in the genre. Barring a few reviews which appeared in the contemporary journals and newspapers, critical attention has seldom been directed to Isvaran's multi-faceted contribution to Indian literature in English. Hence, it is imperative for the sake of the tradition of Indian literature in English to rescue Isvaran from oblivion and ensure him the place that he deserves in the rich heritage of our literature.

The present book makes a pioneering attempt at evaluating Isvaran's creative efforts as a short story writer with special emphasis on his themes and techniques. The work is divided into nine chapters. The first chapter is introductory, concerning itself with the genesis of modern short story, as also the Indian short story in English, and examining Isvaran's place in the growth and development of this genre. The second chapter analyzes the thematic concerns of Isvaran. It particularly notes how most of Isvaran's stories have as their themes an array of religious, ritualistic, social, familial, fantastic and fabulous features that seldom show any aversion to mingling among themselves. The third chapter shows how Isvaran's themes sprout from the contemporary political and social soil. The fourth chapter reveals how Isvaran's genius is marked by a deeper understanding of the nature of his characters in their different relationships in the family as well as in the society. The fifth chapter depicts how religion, which has always been a dominant force, exercising its hold on all spheres of human activity in India, influences the themes of Isvaran's stories. Chapter six concerns itself with some of Isvaran's themes cast in the form of fables, fairy tales, and folk tales. In all such stories he assumes the role of a moral teacher in the tradition of tale-spinners down the ages. Chapter seven discusses how Isvaran's entire system as a story-teller is coloured by the lyrical element. By endowing his prose with poetic rhythm and musical cadence, he explores the narrative possibilities. Chapter eight forms an investigation into the technique, form and style of Isvaran's stories. It examines how in form and technique his stories present an amalgam of the methods employed in the fable, the parable, the epic, the folk tale and the modern well-made short story. Chapter nine, while summing up the various aspects of Isvaran's short stories, considers his position among the Indian English writers of his time.

I should like to place on record my profound gratitude to Dr. K. Venkata Reddy, Professor of English, Sri Krishnadevaraya University, Anantapur (A.P.), who kindled in me an interest in the literary works of Manjeri S. Isvaran, and later guided me in this research project. I am deeply indebted to him for the invaluable suggestions he offered me at every stage of the preparation of this book.

Mrs. Annapurna Isvaran was gracious enough to make available to me both the published and unpublished works of her husband for the present study. Mr. K. Venkataraman, Isvaran's brother-in-law, provided me with sufficient literary and epistolary material on and by Isvaran that helped me in gaining an insight into the literary merit of Isvaran. I am sincerely grateful to both of them.

My regards are due to Professor M.K. Ramachandran Nair (Retd.), N.S.S. College, Ottapalam, for widening the horizons of my perception of literature. I would also like to thank all my colleagues in the Department of English, N.S.S. College, Pandalam, for their warmth and co-operation all along.

Dr. N. Radhakrishnan, Director, Gandhi Smriti and Darshan Samiti, New Delhi, has been an unfailing source of encouragement and inspiration to me throughout my work. I thank him sincerely.

Finally I must put on record my gratitude and appreciation for Prestige Books for bringing out this book expeditiously and so elegantly.

Indian English Short Story and Manjeri S. Isvaran

Indian writers of short fiction in English were neither numerically nor literarily significant until the beginning of the present century. Manjeri S. Isvaran is one of the first Indian writers in English of a recognizable stature to cast his lot with the development of the short story, and he did so at a time when it was yet to find a foothold in the field of Indian-English letters. Before his advent, the short story as a modern art form was mainly the occasional diversion of a novelist.

Isvaran, who published his first collection of short stories, *Naked Shingles* in 1941, is the first Indian writer in English to establish a reputation almost solely on the basis of his achievement in the field of short story. Bankim Chandra Chatterjee, Sarat Chandra Chatterjee, Romesh Chandra Dutt and others who were concerned primarily with novels had sporadically tried their hands at short stories. Rabindra Nath Tagore, to whose credit stand some of the finest short stories in English, was primarily concerned with other literary forms like poems, plays and novels. Though Isvaran's better known contemporaries, Raja Rao, Mulk Raj Anand and R.K. Narayan have authored some inimitable short stories, their reputation rests on their novels, rather than on their short stories.

Isvaran is, in fact, the first among that little band of Indian-English writers who staked their claim to literary reputation on short story. We can hardly ignore his substantial contribution as a poet, but his main focus was on the short story.

To understand Isvaran's art properly and to assess it justly, one has to trace the development of the short story in India and elsewhere, for he is not an isolated phenomenon, but a significant link in the chain of development of the short story as a modern art form. So, an assessment of Isvaran's achievement as a practitioner of the short story makes it imperative to trace his literary ancestry and his indebtedness to his predecessors.

As a literary form and an oral tradition, the short story dates back to pre-historic times. Since the dawn of human civilization it has flourished as an important and engaging social art. The earliest stories mark man's slow emergence from his animal status. The forms of these stories, like the forms of the rituals of primitive man, helped create for him, his history and identity, and were part of the creative impulse that made him consciously human.

All primitive societies, since the invention of language, have had their myths and legends—narratives of how the universe came into being, how humans came, how the tribe emerged and survived through thick and thin, how the heroes fought. That is why "if asked to cite an example of a brief prose narrative, many people call to mind one of the memorable old Testament stories"[1] or the *Upanishads* or the *Jataka Tales.*

What is significant about these tales, and the feature that distinguishes them from the modern short story, is that each tribe considered its tale the gospel, the sacred word. These tales, unlike the modern short story, were not merely make-believe, but belief itself. These stories inevitably bore the halo of some faith, however crude it might be. Moreover we cannot neglect the value of these tales as a means of entertainment. As Ian Reid points out, "We have to look beyond the Hebrew Scriptures to ancient Egypt for the earliest extant stories evidently told for their intrinsic value as entertainment."[2] Though some of these tales appear funny, their purpose is consciously and intensely serious. The fables of Aesop have been popular all over the world as a source of instruction and enjoyment ever since the period of classical Greece. The Middle Ages had their stories in the *Gesta Romanorum*, in Boccaccio's *Decameron* and in Chaucer's *Canterbury Tales*. The Persians had their alluring legends, and the Middle East its gorgeous *Arabian Nights*. As noted by H. E. Bates, "The history of the short story, through its phases of myth and legend, fable and parable, anecdote and pictorial essay, sketch, and even down to what the crudest provincial reporter calls 'a good story,' cannot be measured. The account in Genesis of the conflict between Cain and Abel is a short story; the parable of the prodigal son is a short story and in itself a masterpiece of compression for all time; the stories of Salome, Ruth, Judith and Susannah are all examples of art that was already old, civilized and highly developed some thousands of years before the vogue of Pamela."[3]

Much of the earliest written literatures the world over borrowed heavily from such prehistoric lore. We tend to read such lore: "With nostalgia, moved by the power of things we have lost: the kinship with nature, sense of community, the certainty of belief."[4] The popular imagination in those days did not require realism in the modern literary sense of the term. The audience for these tales loved the marvellous. As

John Hampson observes, "many of the folk tales which entertained mankind in those early ages come down to us as part of our great heritage of culture which is not confined within the bounds of race or creed."[5]

The genesis of Indian tales can be traced back to the *Vedas* and the *Upanishads*, the *Puranas*, the *Panchatantra* and the *Jataka Tales*. These are older than the fables of Aesop and travelled beyond the bounds of the subcontinent to Asia Minor in the North West and China in the North East. The *Mahabharata* and the *Ramayana*, the twin epics, have proved inexhaustible mines from which creative artists of the country have quarried for their material for ages. While assessing the role of the short story in modern Indian literature, M. Rama Rao rightly observes: "We have had in India stories which lie embedded in the hymns of the *Rigveda*, or scattered in the *Upanishads* and the epics, the stories which constitute the *Panchatantra*, the *Hitopadesha*, the *Sukasaptati*, the *Dasakumaracharita* and the *Vetalapanchavimsati* in Sanskrit, the Buddhist *Jataka Tales* in Pali and a host of similar stories in modern Indian languages."[6] These antique tales passing from generation to generation have tempted the great epic poets to stuff into their poetic framework enormous mass of religion, philosophy and polity which are often incongruous with their central theme. Although these tales appear funny, their purpose is intensely serious. Introducing a collection of Indian short stories Shiv K. Kumar comments: "Ingeniously conceived and skilfully structured, most of these stories, both about human beings and animals, offer an inexhaustible source of pleasure even to the contemporary reader."[7] They are tales of practical wisdom and worldly polity or illuminating commentaries on epic and religious myths. We may say with R.K. Narayan, "every story has implicit in it a philosophical or moral significance and our understanding of the distinction between good and evil."[8]

Each place in the vast subcontinent, village and town alike, has tales woven round some deity of its own, at the same time maintaining an unmistakable connection with the great epics in some way or the other. Writers of varying statures in our country have found immense delight in nostalgic harking back to the rich cultural and literary tradition that has come down to them in the form of stories.

Indian literature from the very beginning of its history has been related to the life of the common people. They have not been for the deification of the scholars alone, but an engaging social art, a comprehensive and artistic medium of expression, to benefit the literate and illiterate alike.

Although story-telling is as old as language itself, "the short story as a conscious literary form is younger than most other forms."[9] That is why Susan Lohafer has observed that it is a "relatively young form born of an old, perhaps the very oldest form of literary expression."[10] It has its beginnings in romanticism, in myths and legends and in the supernatural. The great practitioners of this modern art form, like Washington Irving, Gogol, Poe and Hawthorne have dealt in some way with a world different from the ordinary world of mundane fact. From the dawn of human history, the short story has existed as a literary form the world over. Readers as well as writers have found in it a form of fiction which they could manage easily. That is why it existed as a Coeval, Coterminal art form through the history of man, and made Susan Lohafer state, "we may say that storying like dreaming, has always been—and will always be—a very homely part of life." (8)

If the short story formed an integral part of, or an intrusive element in, a larger work in the olden days, now it has gained an independent status with an identity of its own and a justification for itself. It is in this sense that one may maintain that it is a product of the twentieth century. But ever since the beginning of the nineteenth century, short fiction has remained the constant focus with the writers in the West.

Despite its being a new luminary in the literary firmament, the short story has established itself as the most favourite genre among the readers as well as the writers, not because of a happy accident in the literary history but on account of "the amalgam of influences and conditions prevailing in the last quarter of the nineteenth century."[11] Like the novel of the eighteenth century, it is the product of a special confluence of literary, cultural and social forces.

These forces exercised fruitful influence first on the American literary scene, producing the pioneers of American short story like Edgar Allan Poe, Nathaniel Hawthorne, Henry James and a host of others. In the fourth decade of the nineteenth century, the short story developed almost simultaneously in Russia and France. From these countries it gradually spread into other regions of the world. In fact, its spread and popularity in America has been such that Frank O'Connor has termed it America's national art form.

Quantitatively and qualitatively America enjoys the most prominent place vis-a-vis the output of this literary form. It does not mean that the Americans alone have authored the greatest short stories. It only means that no important American writer of fiction has neglected the short form, and in the case of many writers from Hawthorne and Poe to Hemingway and Faulkner, the short story represents a significant part of their literary achievement. In France this literary genre was firmly established in the third decade of the nineteenth century with the proliferation of magazines. However, "the substantial developments came much later: the pastoral freshness of *Daudet's Lettres Dee Mon Moulin* (1869), the cool, meticulous objectivity of Flaubert's *Trois Contest* (1877), and the more styptic naturalism of Maupassant's copious output in the 1880s."[12]

Simultaneously, short story emerged as a literary genre in Russia where Gogol and Turgenev gave it new dimensions. Gogol's contribution to Russian short story is such that Turgenev declares, "We all [have] come out from under Gogol's 'Overcoat.'"[13] This statement of Turgenev shows the seminal importance of "The Overcoat" for later practitioners of the genre. Gogol's tales bear the unmistakable stamp of the folk tradition. Chekhov's place as a writer of short fiction is inestimable. His "ability to convey simultaneously the inner reality and the typicality of characters like Olga in 'The Butterfly' (1894) and Ariadne (in the story of that name first published in 1895) has never been surpassed."[14]

For various reasons its efflorescence was delayed in England where it did not emerge as a distinct literary form until the late eighties. H.E. Bates rightly points out, "the history of the English short story is very brief for the simple reason that before the end of the nineteenth century it had no history." In the course of its progress, the English short story was so profoundly influenced by the Russian, French and American examples that it is impossible to understand its evolution without reference to them.

The variety of this literary genre and the elasticity of its form have made writers of vastly different temperaments and outlooks accept it as the finest and most convenient medium for the communications of their experience of life. The practitioners of this aesthetic form in the West have been intimately connected, especially in its more recent developments, with the social, political and economic upheavals in the community and the authors have focussed attention on their stories on specific problems. There was a great demand for short stories because of the unprecedented proliferation of the newspapers, the development of the magazine and the rapid expansion of the radio and TV network.

The cinema also "helped the evolution of tales complete in themselves both in theme and temperament, yet demanding not much time for their perusal."[15] The diffusion of mass education with the consequential spurt in human curiosity and the increasing tempo and competitive pressure of modern life have given this literary genre its greatest encouragement. As H.E. Bates explains: "One obvious reason for its unique vogue has been the rush of modern life which has made man impatient of the huge tomes, 'the great still books,' as Tennyson called the novels over which readers spent hours in more leisurely ages." (213)

Short fiction is one of the most popular forms of reading today. It has turned out to be an inevitable and integral ingredient of the thousands of magazines all over the world. This popular form of art now covers a wide range thematically and stylistically from the tales of mystery and intrigue, and love and adventure to the more serious type of stories which concern themselves with portraying character, delineating mood, illuminating the atmosphere of a locality, analyzing the complex phases of a situation or considering aspects of certain problems of topical interest. It has, in fact, become a vehicle of creative talent or artistic genius. Its brevity which makes a comparatively less taxing demand on the time of the reader and the possibility of its including all aspects of life and society which the novelist cannot always pay attention to have made the short story a popular genre. Poe, who is "the greatest single influence upon the modern short story," says that it offers "the ideal creative opportunity."[16]

The short story is an art form that defies definition and so "no completely satisfactory definition of a short story has ever been formulated"[17] though "many definitions have been, and always are being, attempted."[18] But the definitions offered differ regarding the exact nature of the short story: "Because individual short stories keep revealing affinities with their forerunners, it is almost impossible to stabilize a definition of the genre; no summary phrase can encapsulate the diversity of possible story types, lengths and approaches. Consequently, no one theory of short story form prevails; most delineations of the art having come from practitioners like Frank O'Connor and H.E. Bates, and being accompanied by clear provisos about their partiality and incompleteness."[19]

Also, the definitions available are too narrow or too broad. All definitions, however, agree upon one point, and that is "the obvious distinctive element in the short story distinguishing it from every other art—its shortness."[20] Perhaps, the most marked traits of short story are "brevity, density, and unity."[21] Ian Reid is of the opinion, "it would be unsatisfactory to make word count the sole criterion. Genre is not arithmetically defined." (10) The significance of brevity lies in inclining "readers to make close verbal connections and perceive relationships of resemblance."[22] Edgar Allan Poe links brevity with intensity. He maintains that emotional or aesthetic arousal can be sustained only for brief periods: "The story culminates in a moment of psychological reaction for the character and of insight for the reader."[23] The definition of the short story given by Sherwood Anderson highlights this point: "The short story is the result of a sudden passion. It is an idea grasped whole as one would pick an apple in an orchard. All of my own short stories have been written at one sitting, many of them under strange enough circumstances. There are these glorious moments, these pregnant hours, and I remember such hours as a man remembers the first kiss got from woman loved."[24] Sean O'Faolin considers it "a more personal genre than the novel. It is the kernel of the matter in hand as the writer sees it. The writer need not be explicit." (57) Wells has defined the short story as "any piece of short fiction that could be read in half an hour."[25]

According to Brander Mathews, the short story "deals with a single character, a single situation, a single emotion or a series of emotions called forth by a single situation."[26] Somerset Maugham holds: "It is not hard to state what Poe meant by a good short story. It is a piece of fiction dealing with a single incident, material or spiritual, that can be read at a sitting; it is original, it must sparkle, excite or impress and it must have unity of effect or impression."[27] A short story writer "must be concerned with a few heightened moments, perhaps only a single one,"[28] which he glorifies and immortalizes.

All these definitions agree on certain vital characteristics, though they differ in certain others. Some of them are too restricting and put the short story form into a rigid frame, that inevitably hampers its freedom of movement, so that it does not include, as it must, certain experiments in the genre which do not conform to a rigid pattern.

The divergences in the attempts to define the short story make us aware that it is safer to examine its possibilities and limitations than to try to define it in precise terms. Perhaps the most significant limitation and strength of the short story is its brevity. A practitioner of this genre paints miniatures. He confines himself to a small canvas, a limited number of characters, a restricted number of settings and a short space of time.

The infinite possibilities of the genre are, in fact, the outgrowth of its limitations. As the story is short, the writer has to condense his material most effectively. All great practitioners of this art form have believed that the finest short stories are closer in technique to poetry. It can focus on a single character or a small set of characters. Thus, the story emerges from the heart of a situation. Most significant of all is its unity—a singleness of effect: "The modern story is likely to find its unity in its thematic materials—in building to a single flash of insight that suddenly reveals whole biographies and histories, like a streak of lightning, illuminating the countryside. Some writers will deliberately weave together seemingly unrelated characters or episodes or styles, but, if skilfully done, the subterranean connections will make these disparate materials suddenly coalesce and fuse into a deeper kind of unity—a unity of idea or spirit or essence."[29] Thus, the guiding principle of the short story is its unity. It concentrates on a single character, in a single situation, at a single moment.

The Indian English short story is a little over hundred years old now. The first Indian English short story collection, *Realities of Indian Life: Stories Collected from the Criminal Reports of India* by Shoshee Chunder Dutt was published in London in 1885. In the same year appeared the collection *The Times of Yore: Tales from Indian History* by Shoshee Chunder Dutt and Sourindra Mohan Tagore. In 1886 and 1887 two collections of stories were published by P.V. Ramaswami Raju: *The Tales of Sixty Mandarins* and *Indian Fables*. Khetrapal Chakravarti published in Calcutta a collection, *Sarada and Hingana: Tales Descriptive of Indian Life*, in 1895, followed by *Stories of Indian Christian Life* in 1898 published in Madras by Kamala Sathyanathan. Rajam Iyer published a few stories in 1896 and 1898. Despite their acceptance of a new form of self-expression, these writers tended to make their stories philosophical, keeping the tradition of ancient Indian tales. It is not to be forgotten that a few writers followed the great masters of the West in writing stories of horror and suspense.

The stories of writers like Rajam Iyer were a rework of mythological and allegorical tales. A study of these early short stories in English reveals that they do not have any "striking features of intrinsic merit, either in narrative technique or in characterization."[30]

The first Indian short story writer in English with a considerable output is Comella Sorabjee, a woman lawyer of Calcutta. Her four collections of short stories are: *Love and Life behind the Purdah* (1901), *Sunbabies: Studies in the Child Life of India* (1904), *Between the Twilights: Being Studies of Indian Women by One of Themselves* (1909) and *Indian Tales of the Great Ones among Men, Women and Bird People* (1916). These stories deal with life as it was lived by the Hindus and the Parsis of the upper and lower classes of the period.

The short story, during the last decade of the nineteenth century and the first decade of the present century, was mostly a rework of folk tales and legends with a strong element of didacticism and sentimentalism. As C.V. Venugopal observes: "these stories have but a historical importance, although credit could be given to them for the fact that their simple narratives actually underline the folk tale form, a form which has been so well exploited later by such noted writers as Raja Rao and Anand."[31]

Notable short story collections which appeared in the first two decades of the present century are S.M. Natesa Sastri's *Indian Folk-Tales* (1908), Dwijendra Nath Neogi's *Sacred Tales of India* (1916), A.

Madhavaiah's *Short Stories by Kusika* (1960) and Sunita Devi's *Bengal Dacoits and Tigers* (1916) and *Beautiful Moghul Princesses.* (1918)

The Gandhian era witnessed an accelerated pace in the development of the short story as an art form. The revolutionary fervour that characterized the social, political and moral movements of the period are refreshingly mirrored in the literature of that period.

Writers of all statures of the mid-century developed a social consciousness to which they gave artistic expression in their works. Despite this consciousness, the works of many of the contemporaries of Isvaran bear overtly the stamp of parables and fables or a tinge of allegory to make out a moral or to make a nice point of metaphysics clear to the understanding of the common man.

A.S.P. Ayyer, K.N. Nagarajan, A. Madhaviah, S. K. Chettur and G.K. Chettur took to the short story form with great zeal. Ayyer's collections, *Indian After-Dinner Stories, Tales of Ind, Three Famous Tales* and *Jolly Old Tales of Ind*, contain stories that share the dictional simplicity and charm of the *Jataka Tales* and the *Panchatantra*. T.L. Natesan who wrote under the pseudonym, 'Sankar Ram,' brought out two volumes of short stories—*The Children of Kaveri* (1927) and *Creatures All* (1933). Stories in these collections present artistic pictures in all their simplicity and grandeur. His style is marked with straightforwardness and good humour, signifying a definite advance in the direction of old rustic realism which had a fascination for Isvaran too. K.S. Venkataramani brought out two collections of short stories—*Paper Boats* (1921) and *Jatadharan and Other Stories* (1937). They are authentic portraits of South Indian life and character in their serious and vivacious, human and humorous aspects.

Tagore, the great spiritual and literary influence of the time, wrote his short stories originally in Bengali and later translated them into English. Most of these stories furnish deep studies in human relations within the large frame of rural life. He, however, does not neglect totally the city life. His stories are peopled with men and women of all ages and of all types in various domestic and social situations. Tagore, who was highly sensitive to the changes taking place in the country—the rise of nationalism, the movements of social and religious reforms, the changing pattern of economy and the development of education after the western models, was also conscious of their deeper impacts.

Artistically commendable stories were written during the Gandhian era. Several volumes of stories by writers of repute like Raja Rao, Mulk Raj Anand, K.S. Venkataramani, A.S.P. Ayyer and S. Nagarajan appeared during this period and these stories were mostly in conformity with the standards of the genre elsewhere. However, Manjeri S. Isvaran was the "most productive of Indian short story writers of the period,"[32] and "one of the pioneers of this emergence."[33]

Isvaran embodies the forces that are very significant for an understanding of the way the short story genre has developed as a distinct artistic form in Indian English literature. The amalgam of influences and conditions prevailing in the first half of the present century, especially in short fiction, is distinctly discernible in his work.

Isvaran is the first Indian short story writer in English to examine this genre as an ancient and enduring form of art and what is more, to put forward a considered opinion of what a modern short story should be. His attempt at expressing a theory of short story shows how seriously he regarded it as an art. Harmonizing inspiration and conscious art enabled him to formulate clearly a theory of short fiction.

It is interesting to note that his theoretical formulations and critical assessments of the short story as an art form came out only after the publication of his major short stories. In his introduction to *A Madras Admiral*, his last collection, *No Ankletbells for Her*, John Hampson observes: "The short story has roots which go back deep into the ancient past linking ourselves, who get our stories through the medium of radio, film and printing press, with those who gathered round eager audience for the teller of tales." (vii) Isvaran's short stories which go back deep into the past inculcate the culture and tradition of Indian art and literature from the pre-Vedic period. He is also very well aware of the various stages of the growth of this literary genre the world over. Hampson further observes: "Many of the folk-tales which entertained mankind in those early ages have come down to us as part of our great heritage of culture, a culture which is not confined within the bounds of race or creed." (vii)

It seems that the term, short story, seen in the *Vedas* and the *Upanishads* is designed in such a way that the philosophical insight ingrained in them is made comprehensible by the common people. Commenting on the *Mahabharata* and the *Ramayana*, Isvaran observes: "The epic bard hummed the heroic measures of Valmiki and Vyasa, and throngs of the learned as well as the lay sat listening to him at the sacrificial sessions. This entertaining and edifying recital was continued by the ubiquitous Kathak and the bhat; the Kirtankar added music and the Chakyar, the mime."

On the didactic element of the ancient Indian tales Isvaran comments: "The Indian story-teller was as fertile in tales inculcating practical wisdom and worldly polity as in illuminating epic and religious myth."[35] An integral part of, or intrusive element in, a large work in the olden days, the short story has gained now an independent status with an identity of its own. The forces which nourished the growth and development of it the world over have exercised their influence on the development of this genre in India though a little differently. Tracing the origin and development of the short story, Isvaran observes:

> In the contemporary Indian scene, the story, more particularly the short story as an art form, has become very popular in the country's several major languages, and also with those who use English as their vehicle of expression. The innate Indian predilection for the tale has, as it were, been revivified by contact with Western literature whose fiction, more than any other genre, has exerted an extensive influence on the writers of about the last three decades here. In the West the story has been intimately connected, especially in its more recent developments, with the social, political, and economic upheavals in the community, and authors have focussed attention, in their stories, on specific problems. This characteristic of the modern short story, whether British, American or European, is also evident in its Indian counterpart and it is therefore, germane to consider what role the story-teller in India has to play in the moulding of the new life with which this ancient country is now seething.[36]

In Isvaran's hands, Indian short story in English gained a new vitality, a new design and a certain quality of transparency. He embodies the forces that are crucial to the understanding of the way the genre has developed in the subcontinent. Hence, the enormous significance of Isvaran's own views on the growth and development of modern short story.

However modern be the short story, Isvaran feels, it is rooted in the ancient culture and civilization. It is no wonder, therefore, if he looks back to the classical Indian literature for moral reflections in the cast of simple narratives and the typical characterization. Interestingly a similar view has been expressed by a modern critic, Valerie Shaw, when she says that the short story "has a unique ability to preserve and at any time to recall its mixed origins in fable, anecdote, fairy story and numerous other forms."[37]

Isvaran thinks that the culture of a people is intimately related to the creative endeavours of short story. In "The Indian Writer in English," he writes: "Culture is creative: it cannot be produced to order, it is the fundamental with which the family keeps its good manners. It manifests itself in innumerable ways: in the endeavours and endurances of humanity. And it is these that a writer has to reflect in his work, staying deep-rooted in his traditional past."[38] This is true of Isvaran's own creative endeavours in the field of Indian short story in English.

Isvaran had a very broad conception of short story. It has a vast scope and function like many other established forms of literature. In its thematic concerns and technical virtuosity, it can be of different modes of literature. This is driven home to us when he says: "A short story can be a fable or a parable, real or fantasy, a true presentation or a parody, sentimental or satirical, serious in intent, or a light-hearted diversion."[39]

As regards the source material and its artistic treatment, Isvaran's view synchronizes with the dramatic practice of Shakespeare. Like Shakespeare, Isvaran is of the view that a creative writer can borrow material freely from any source as long as he can make it his own by giving it his own artistic treatment. This is made clear when Isvaran says: "There is no writer who has not lifted some material from another, and also there is no writer worth the name, who has not been able to present it in a fresh setting and shape."[40] For Isvaran, inventiveness in the treatment of the source material is "the first and main basis of a story."[41] He thinks, "the very novelty of a story is its appeal and infinite are the variations that the story-teller can introduce."[42]

Isvaran has definite views on the making of a writer and his characteristics. Like Ben Jonson and Milton, he believes in the 'perseverance' on the part of the writer. While subscribing to the view that "the real writer comes into being because he has the itch to write,"[43] Isvaran lays stress on the pains that the creative writer should take to shape himself into a good writer. He says: "Good writing is born of years of perseverance, the easiest to read has been the hardest to write."[44]

A writer is shaped as much by the contemporaneity as by tradition. Naturally, the story-teller is deeply indebted to the contemporary world. Isvaran says:

> The story-teller, today, cannot abstract himself from the contemporary world, he cannot also absolve himself of the role of the seer—one who sees truth and inner harmony on which things are strung together. His voice now, more than at any other time, should not be that of destructive exposition, but of peace and good will, "winning the world as rose or lily wins it," and should go on winning it with the marvel of his intelligent heart, seeing other hearts unite in sympathy, shared wonder and the joy of beauty. He is the Ancient Mariner, and the world the Wedding Guest.[45]

Like T.S. Eliot, Isvaran believes in the need for the impersonality on the part of the writer. In his "Tradition and Individual Talent," Eliot says: "The progress of an artist is a continual self-sacrifice, a continual extinction of personality."[46] Isvaran seems to echo Eliot when he expresses almost the same view in an essay, "The Writer," published in *Swatantra*:

> First of all the writer must possess some measure of impersonality. Self-consciousness and impersonality, it would seem, are inseparable in principle. The writer deals with character and to understand character, he needs the impersonality of a scientist, or something like it. He may even be impersonal in regard to himself, as was one of the greatest writers, Leo Tolstoy. Further, impersonality is an essential companion. A man can have sympathy without being impersonal, but in this case sympathy is a partisan emotion. How could Dostoevsky, for example, write about the lowest human beings without exciting in the reader any emotion except pity, if he had not been impersonal?

Isvaran insists on the emotional involvement of the reader in the stories without putting aside the moral idea to be grasped intellectually in good story. He writes: "Through the incident and its artistic treatment the writer is endeavouring to place before the reader some problem and its solution. The short story inevitably tries to bring home some lesson, but in quite unobtrusive manner. No real author ever appears to teach, but all great authors have always been leaders of epochs."[47]

Lastly, Isvaran suggests the means and ways of making a short story 'memorable.' If the short story is to stand the test of time and survive to posterity, "it must catch the eternal in the casual, invest a moment with the immensity of time."[48] It may be noted that Katherine Mansfield had similar views regarding the nature of the short story. Nariman Hormasji rightly points out: "All Life was not Miss Mansfield's realm: a mere part of a segment—a slice."[49] P. Obula Reddy who has made an in-depth study of the short stories of Katherine Mansfield observes: "The stories of Katherine Mansfield, however, are more than moments, instants and gleams of life, she has given them touches of eternity."[50]

To conclude, the short story as a conscious literary form is young, though as a literary expression, it can be traced back to the dawn of civilization. From being a homely part of everyday life, it has evolved into a form of deliberate art that aims as much at edification as at entertainment. The nations of the world, the chief among them being America, Russia, France and India, have had writers who have substantially contributed to the qualitative improvement and quantitative growth of the genre. Its thematic variety and formal elasticity have endeared it to readers all over the world.

Manjeri Isvaran was the most prolific of the short story writers of his period. In his deft hands, the genre developed into a distinct art form in Indian English literature. The characteristic flavour of a cultural slice of essentially Indian ethos emanates from his stories. An attempt is made in the following chapters to make a close study of the thematic concerns and technical virtuosities of Isvaran's short stories in English.

NOTES

1. Ian Reid, *The Short Story* (London: Methuen), p. 15.
2. *Ibid.*, pp. 15-16.
3. *The Modern Short Story from 1809 to 1953* (London: Robert Hale, 1988), p. 13.
4. Wilfred Stone, Nancy Huddleston Packer et al, ed., *The Short Story: An Introduction* (New York: McGraw Hill, 1976), p. 1.
5. Introduction, *No Ankletbells for Her* (Madras: Mitra, 1949), p. vii.
6. "The Short Story in Modern Indian Literature," *Fiction and the Reading Public in India* (Mysore: University of Mysore, 1967), p. 216.
7. Introduction, *Modern Indian Short Stories* (Delhi: OUP, 1983), p. vii.
8. "The World of the Story-Teller," *Fiction and the Reading Public in India.*
9. James E. Miller, Jr. and Bernice Slot, ed., *The Dimensions of Short Story: A Critical Anthology* (New York: Dodd, Mead, 1972), p. 511.
10. *Coming to Terms with the Short Story* (Baton Rouge: Louisiana State UP, 1983), p. 8.
11. Valerie Shaw, *The Short Story: A Critical Introduction* (London: Longman, 1983), p. 29.
12. Reid, p. 24.
13. Qtd. Frank O'Connor, *The Lonely Voice: A Study of the Short Story* (London: Methuen, 1963), p. 14.
14. Valerie Shaw, p. 120.
15. *Fiction and the Reading Public in India,* p. 213.
16. Randal Stewart and Dorothy Bethurun, *The Classic American Fiction* (New York: Scott, Foresman, 1954), p. 3.
17. Harry Shaw and Douglas Beiment, *Reading the Short Story* (New York: Harper, 1941), p. 1.
18. *The Modern Short Story from 1809 to 1953*, p. 16.
19. *The Short Story: A Critical Introduction*, p. 20.
20. Sean O'Faolin, *The Short Story* (London: Collins, 1948), p. 37.
21. *The Dimensions of Short Story: A Critical Anthology*, pp. 509-19.
22. Suzanna Hunder Brown, "Tess and Tess: An Experiment in Genre," *Modern Fiction Studies, The Modern Short Story,* Spring 1982, Vol. 28, No. 1, p. 39.
23. Qtd. *Ibid*, p. 30.

24. Robert Gorham Davis, ed., *Ten Modern Masters: An Anthology of the Short Story* (New York: Harcourt, Brace and World, 1953), p. 533.
25. Qtd. H.E. Bates, p. 16.
26. Mary Rohrberger, *Hawthorne and the Modern Short Story: A Study in Genre* (The Hague: Mouton, 1966), p. 12.
27. *Points of View* (1959: London: Heinemann, 1960), p. 155.
28. James B. Hall and Joseph Land, ed., *The Short Story* (New York: Macmillan, 1956), p. 2.
29. *The Dimensions of Short Story: A Critical Anthology*, p. 511.
30. C.V. Venugopal, *The Indian Short Story in English* (Bareilly: Prakash, n.d), p. 22.
31. C.V. Venugopal, "The Indian Short Story: A Brief Survey," *Perspectives on Indian Fiction in English* (New Delhi: Abhinav, 1985), p. 226.
32. M.K. Naik, Introduction, *The Indian Short Story: A Representative Anthology* (New Delhi: Arnold-Heinemann, 1984), p. 20.
33. K.S. Venkataramani, Introduction, *Naked Shingles* (Madras: Devi Press, 1941), p. vii.
34. Isvaran, Book Review, *Stories from the Indian Classics*, Selected and retold by V.S. Naravane (Typescript), p. 116.
35. "By Way of Preface," *A Madras Admiral* (Madras: Dhanus, 1959), p. vii.
36. *Loc. cit.*
37. *Short Story: A Critical Introduction*, p. 20.
38. *Swarajya*, 21 Sept. 1957, p. 10.
39. "The Role of the Story-Teller in the Modern World," *The Aryan Path*, Dec. 1957, p. 537.
40. *A Madras Admiral*, p. ix.
41. *Loc. cit.*
42. *Loc. cit.*
43. "The Writer and the Public," Typescript.
44. "Learning the Craft: Lessons from the Masters, *Swaraja*, 10 Nov. 1956, p. 7.
45. *A Madras Admiral*, p. ix.
46. *English Critical Texts*, ed. D.J. Enright and Ernest De Chickera (London: Oxford UP, 1964), p. 296.
47. "The Role of the Story Teller in the Modern World," p. 537.
48. *Ibid.*
49. *Katherine Mansfield: An Appraisal* (London: Collins, 1967), p. 104.
50. "The Short Stories of Katherine Mansfield: A Study in Themes and Techniques," diss., S.K. University, Anantapur, 1987, p. 239.

Isvaran's Thematic Concerns

Of all the essential and vitally inter-related ingredients of a story, the theme is, perhaps, the most difficult to define. Nevertheless, attempts have been made to define it. Wilfred Stone, Nancy Huddleton Packer and Robert Hoopes write: "After pleasure or pain, excitement or perplexity caused by the story had receded, the reader is left with a residue, a distillation, that we call theme."[1] So the theme is something that emerges from the obscure system the writer provides. In a broad sense, a theme "may simply be a characteristic view of life that pervades a story."[2] It is the "general vision of life or the more explicit proposition about human experience that literature conveys."[3] Harry Shaw maintains that the theme tells "some truth about life or human behaviour."[4]

These concepts of theme in short fiction suggest that short story, like other fictional forms, expresses the values of a writer and his understanding of the human condition. The story in its entirety thus expands the theme. A story is not a mere narration of events or the depiction of a situation. The event or situation in some may echo that in the lives of the readers. This is caused by shaping the events in such a way as to extract a meaning out of it. This meaning is sometimes a moral or a philosophical idea or something that illumines life. As Lynn Alterbernd and Leslie L. Lewis remark: "Not all stories are profoundly philosophic, but they either add to our knowledge of life or else give us a fresh, or subtly qualified, or vividly dramatized idea."[5]

Thus, theme involves the controlling idea or philosophical subject which largely determines the selection and organization of the material in a story. This vision or idea in an ideal situation sprouts from the soil of the writer's experience. The view of Henry James on how the themes of a story-teller evolve from his experiences illustrates this point. He writes: "Experience is never limited, and it is never complete; it is an immense sensibility, a kind of huge spider web of the finest silken threads suspended in the chamber of consciousness and catching every air-borne particles in its tissue, it is the very atmosphere of the mind, and when the mind is imaginative, much more when it happens to be that of a man of genius—it takes to itself the faintest hints of life, it converts the very pulses of the air into revelations."[6]

A good story is seldom the illustration of an idea. It creates an image of life by which significance emerges from experience. This is driven home to us when Cleanth Brooks and Robert Penn Warren observe: "It is the idea, the significance, the interpretation of persons and events, the pervasive and unifying view of life which is embodied in the total narrative. It is . . . what we are to make of human experience rendered in the story. And what we make of such human experience always involves, directly or indirectly, some comment on values in human nature and human conduct, on the good and bad, on the true and the false, some conception of what the human place is in the world."[7]

A study of the themes of fiction has a direct bearing on the personal experiences of the artist, for every writer is shaped by the social, political, economic, religious, moral and cultural forces as well as by his sense of tradition and history. His themes, forms, assumptions and even his rhetorical styles are determined and shaped by these forces that make up the environment in which he lives and to which he responds. So, the close relation between creative effort and the historical situation from which it emerges has become a vital clue to any serious attempt at literary evaluation.

Isvaran's themes are "of a surprising and pleasant variety."[8] His fictional world has been built around plots drawn from legend, myth, folklore, nature, and contemporary socio-economic and political life. It is a world as complex as art and as baffling as life. Each story is an experiment in theme and technique. Consequently, it has been found that the classification of his tales into certain groups on the basis of themes is not an easy task. In fact, the key to the understanding of his fictional themes lies in an objective assessment of his varied experiences in relation to the materials that go into the making up of his stories.

The observations and experiences of early life in the rural atmosphere of an orthodox family, the vast erudition acquired in an entirely different urban environment as a student, impressions gained through extensive travel, association with eminent men of letters, and insights earned by profound reflection throughout his life enabled Isvaran to develop a philosophy and outlook on life which find harmonious expression in his stories. His experiences and insights lead him into metaphysical realms where good and evil are in conflict, which, understood in the proper way, leads to thorough purification, even if it involves a tragic end for some of his protagonists.

Isvaran's thematic base is the landscape and socio-scape of the region that he frequented in his early years or his own vision moulded by his personal experiences. One cannot, however, deny the fact that his significance as a creative writer transcends the apparently inevitable limitations of region, religion, race, and even his themes.

While commenting upon the literary merits of the fictional writings of Elizabeth Bowen, Isvaran quotes her words: "Nothing can happen nowhere. The locale of the happening always colours the happenings and often, to a degree shapes it. Plot having pre-decided what is to happen, scenes must be so found, so chosen, as to give the happening the desired force."[9] Scene, according to Bowen, is inside the artist's conscious power. Isvaran as a writer maintains a similar view. Like his great contemporaries R.K. Narayan, Raja Rao and Mulk Raj Anand, Isvaran orchestrates themes which belong to his age and place, themes which recur with variations in his poems and short stories. The tales have their inception in a landscape which is either real or nostalgically remembered. Isvaran's most sympathetic presentations of country life are based either on his childhood memories of Malabar as that of "Gold on His Lips" and "The Stolen Jackfruit" or certain parts of Tamil Nadu as the locale of the stories "Jowramma" and "The Serpent Gem." The major portion of the action of "Immersion" transpires in rural Malabar. In "Naked Shingles" Isvaran depicts the life of the fisher folk of the sea coast of Madras.

Isvaran's descriptions comprise an admirable admixture of landscapes, or more rapid, but always vivid sketches, all vibrant with life. The landscapes depicted by Isvaran are seen to be inseparably related to the lives of his characters. Isolated from the characters, they have no significance. He establishes a correlation between the natural and the fictional effortlessly. The topographical description introduces the reader to a scene unique in landscape and atmosphere.

The locale chosen for the stories is recognizably Indian. Local colour is demonstrably the life of Isvaran's stories which transcend the purely regional. He has portrayed with great fidelity the South Indian scene in its manifold variety. With photographic accuracy he records the local topography, architecture, manners, customs, rituals, superstitions and character types. Isvaran's local colour stories present a type of realism, if realism can be defined as a graphic delineation of actual life. Commenting upon Isvaran as a short-story writer, D. Anjaneyulu writes: "Isvaran is essentially a realist in his approach to the art of the short story. He has a keen eye for detail and he depicts everything as he sees it through the wonderful colour camera of his mind—the beauty of a rural landscape, the squalor of a street, a scene in the city, the cosiness of the bedroom in a happy middle class home, or the crowded discomforts of a third class railway compartment. He is perhaps closer in his realism to D.H. Lawrence, Katherine Mansfield and Guy de Maupassant than, say, Ernest Hemingway, John Steinbeck or Gorky and Dostoevsky. Whether it be the struggle of the Rickshawallah to make a precarious living, that of the farmhand, the fisherman or the beggar, it is brought to the reader in all its vividness and intensity, but there is no attempt at causing a revulsion in him, by indulging in melodrama at the least provocation as is the habit with many of the progressive writers."[10] Isvaran's realism is concerned with epitomizing the ordinary activities of the middle class and lower class people by closely observing and recording their most typical behaviour. He in fact, expresses a sense of truth embodied in a personal vision of certain aspects of human behaviour.

As the socio-political, religious and cultural strands in the life of Isvaran's characters are inextricably intertwined, it is inadvisable though not impossible to classify his themes into water-tight compartments. It is a well known fact that in almost all classics of Indian literature written before the impact of Western civilization, authors assume the truth as dictated by Hindu religious faith. In these literatures religion and imagination are integrated making culture an offshoot of religion and maintaining its unity all through the long history of the nation.

Isvaran lived through two world wars. He watched Indian nationalism assuming shape and taking very decisive turns. He witnessed the changing patterns of economic development in the country, the emergence of a new outlook on education and the birth of a growing consciousness of internationalism. The nationalist movement which had caught the imagination of the entire nation was a tremendous inspiration to Indian writers. The various aspects of the great social and political transformation that the nation was experiencing under the powerful spiritual guidance and political leadership of Mahatma Gandhi were a great inspiration to the writers, small and great, of the country. P.P. Mehta rightly observes: "Gandhiji's impact on Indian writers was direct and widespread. Apart from its political repercussions it was both moral and intellectual and at once inhibitive and liberating. Gandhiji stripped urban life and 'elegance' of their pretensions and emphasized that religion without compassion and culture without conscience were worthless. He transfigured the image of India and turned national idealism from its futile adulation of the past to face the reality of India as she was poor, starving and hopeless, but with an untapped potential of unlimited possibilities."[11]

The manifestation of the proliferation of the Gandhian ideal in both urban and rural India is seen in almost all the works of Isvaran's contemporaries. In the words of Meenakshi Mukherjee: "The most potent force behind the whole movement, the Mahatma, is a recurring presence in these novels and he is used in different ways to suit the design of each writer. He has been treated variously as an idea, a myth, a symbol, a tangible reality and a benevolent human being. In a few novels he appears in person, in most others his is an invisible presence."[12] Indian nationalism, though primarily a political gesture, was basically a social and cultural movement which had assumed vital significance for the Indian writers in English.

In the novels and short stories written during this period, we find the "East-West" theme operating as the conflict between modern industrialization and urban life on the one hand and Indian rural life on the other. In his essay entitled "Indian Writing," Isvaran writes:

> It is a mistake to think that Indian nationalism is an indigenous growth. It would have been unthinkable without the cultural contact with the West; it was not a return to pre-British days, it was very definitely a phenomenon arising out of an acquaintance with certain elements of European civilization with Ruskin, with Tolstoy, with European voices raised against the bourgeois character of a western nineteenth century civilization with the re-discovery and the re-appraisal of India's past by European scholars.[13]

Indian nationalism thus was not simply the offshoot of a political upsurge. On the one hand, it was a scientific attitude hitherto unknown to the land and, on the other, a deep attachment to and regard for the purer spiritual and cultural tradition of India. Ideas of progress and social change came to blend with the best of India's cultural past. Spiritual leaders, intellectuals and social reformers all over India accepted the path of the Mahatma, and India was moving ahead for deeper social and cultural changes. The demand of the time was to be that an Indian writer was under a sacred obligation to get involved in the national movement.

The multifarious manifestations of the nationalist movement figure prominently in the major works of the contemporaries of Isvaran. As Meenakshi Mukherjee points out: "The struggle for independence became one such unifying force in the two decades preceding the actual achievement of political freedom, and no novelist living in or dealing with this period could avoid writing about it."[14]

Isvaran keenly observed the development of the short story in relation to the social, political and economic upheavals. As a writer he felt that he had a role to play in the moulding of the national life. Like his contemporaries, Isvaran too developed a deep sense of nationalism. He felt: "The independence movement in India was not merely a political struggle, but an all-pervasive emotional experience for all Indians in the nineteen twenties and thirties. No Indian writer, writing in these decades or writing about them could avoid reflecting this upsurge in his work."[15]

The social, political and intellectual atmosphere in which Isvaran functioned in the formative years of his life, and the years that matured him as a man and as a writer were years that saw the rise of Indian nationalism. He was a close witness to its social impact. "Indian national movement," observes Isvaran, "brought in every field of creative activity a fine enthusiasm. . . . The national movement grew along with the national press, authorship, and journalism, banding together in the unremitting struggle for freedom."[16] Isvaran was well aware not only of the social and political scenario but also of the literary and the cultural developments brought about by India's cultural contact with the West, during the decades preceding India's attainment of political freedom. He comments: "The social milieu and the political scene in India—thanks to the external forces—are at present in a state of flux. The rapid multiplication of periodicals and the literary interest evinced by the daily press have gained the widest possible public for the current story teller."[17]

The significant impact of Gandhism, apart from the theme of nationalist movement, at the literary level is that of a shift from romanticism to realism. This feature is more conspicuous in Isvaran's poems than in his prose fiction. Life in Madras, the centre of national awakening in the South, provided Isvaran with thrilling experiences particularly because of his association with the daily press and personal friendship with Indian celebrities like M.K. Ramakotiswara Rau, an ardent nationalist who was imprisoned several times for his active role in the national struggle for freedom, V.S. Sreenivasa Sastri who was Gokhale's friend and Gandhiji's exact contemporary and a highly valued friend, M. Chalapathi Rau and a number of Indians who took up active roles in the national struggle.

The South India of the third, fourth and the fifth decades of the present century proved a major source of literary material for Isvaran. Out of it he created a world of his own as varied, complex and complete as the original one. It cannot be denied that he had in mind a world dominated mainly by the British imperialist forces and bureaucracy, but at the background of his tales we see the unmistakable presence of the middle and the lower classes.

However, it is surprising to note that while Indian national unity, integration, and the impact of the world wars were recurring themes in the writings of Isvaran's contemporaries, he himself had chosen the theme of national movement only in one of his short stories, "Between Two Flags." Perhaps he was aware of the too limited scope of the short story to enable his characters to establish their full identity as in the case of the novels like Raja Rao's *Kanthapura*, R.K. Narayan's *Waiting for the Mahatma*, and Mulk Raj Anand's *Untouchable*.

Isvaran's fictional world is peopled with persons of all ages belonging to the middle and lower classes of the south India. These characters are presented in different social and family relationships. Like the world of Isvaran's contemporaries, Isvaran's society too is male-dominated, but his sympathy is always with his women characters. He does not treat them as inferior—they are virtuous, graceful and generous in forgiving the wrongs perpetuated on them by their husbands. Commenting on Isvaran's characters, C.V. Venugopal observes: "Marital unions are invariably psychologically well-matched, with the wife a devoted worshipper of her husband who in turn is considerate and affectionate. No woman is a coquette, no husband a philanderer! Bliss it would certainly be to be merely alive in the Manjeri middle class world! It is in his descriptions of the men and women of the lower class, however, that Isvaran is to be seen at his best as a story teller. Here is unbridled, uninhibited exposure of life. One might almost say, 'Here's God's plenty.'"[18]

The diverse aspects of feminine psychology are revealed in the stories with clear insight. The only middle-class woman that Isvaran draws as a dominating type is Lakshmi in the story, "The Miracle of the Door." In the story the characters and episodes are like those of a fable rather than of a modern short story. However, Isvaran tries to present in the story a social type: "Always exacting and unsatisfied, with the firm grip of a male on life, she drew into herself all the masculinity of her husband, leaving him to develop the docility and drowsiness which properly should have been hers."[19]

In the portrayal of such a character as Lakshmi, Isvaran seems to have a moral purpose. She has to compensate for her vices even after death. The characters often represent essential truths about human beings. This truth lies in carefully chosen significant moments. In contrast to Gangi, a trusting and devoted girl all tenderness towards her husband even after knowing his infatuation for another woman, Isvaran introduces in the story "The Motorman" a woman, Vallachi, "a perfect she animal,"[20] who "knew how to noose a young fellow." (59) Yet another archetype of ill-disposed women presented in the stories is the stepmother who makes her appearance in "Kolu" and "No Birds Sing." In "Kolu" she emerges as "a young woman whose eyes detonated anger" (72) towards three children, two girls and a boy, whereas in "No Birds Sing" she is the "embittered Irulayi and her yearning femininity which was starved, rebelled against the unmaleness of her man in mingled contempt and disgust, and hated his children whom it regarded as imps mocking her sterility."[21] She later becomes "the proprietress of a pleasure house" (60) and is sentenced to six months' imprisonment for it and before she completes the term of imprisonment she goes mad.

Isvaran's most familiar type of women characters are doting mothers, loving sisters, devoted wives, and pious, loving, and conservative grandmothers. They are given the full realization in his stories as ideal characters. However, the nagging wives, alluring and petty women, cruel mothers-in-law and stepmothers are relegated to the background as subordinate characters, who quite often present a contrast to his ideal women.

Isvaran's theme invariably centres round human relationships and what they may symbolize. He places his characters in milieus that demand multi-faceted relationships. To him family relationship, however, is the fundamental part of life. He does not, of course, limit his treatment of the family to his own personal experiences. His wide observation and equally wide sympathies preclude any such exclusive viewpoint. "By and large, it is always the drama of human life in the intimacy of personal relations at home, round the street corner, at the temple festival, in the village market, by the seashore or out at sea that fascinates him. The passing convulsions of public life provide him at best with only the backdrop for some of his short stories, but never the main substance."[22] Isvaran's stories show the depth of understanding of human situations. He does not deal with life in its length and breadth. His outlook is fragmentary, it does not reflect the vision and imagination of total life.

The variety of characters and the situations in which they are made to reveal themselves in Isvaran's stories are really amazing. His characters range from children to old men and women and are presented in the context of different domestic relationships. Even the characters in *Fancy Tales* and other fable-like stories take on traits that are essentially human.

In tracing the interaction between the physical environment and man's inner world, Isvaran shows a rare grasp of the urges that motivate the human being. He is at his best while depicting the reality of human emotion and of the shifts in individual consciousness as it struggles towards identity and meaning. He introduces states of consciousness which are very significant in plumbing the depths of human mind and interpreting their life, and the deeper principles and forces that lie behind their apparently superficial behaviour. This inevitably makes it necessary to penetrate beyond surface impressions and reach at the realms of a deeper truth by means of the great complex of events and surface data. Isvaran thinks that a story is great only when it reveals the inner reality.

The major characters in Isvaran's serious stories are endowed with sincere feelings and mutual good-will, but life remains tragic, not because of the presence of any adversary, but because of the complex circumstances which seem to lie beyond the control of human beings. This happens as a result of accident or chance caused by a force acting independently and capriciously outside human will. Isvaran believes that everything that happens in nature and in human life which is a part of nature has reason. He recognizes that man's deeds, his 'guilt' or 'sin' bears the responsibility for his future. "All the same, the typical Indian predilection for a happy or conciliatory ending always governs Isvaran's stories."[23] Despite an undertone of melancholy in most of his stories, he is optimistic about the final outcome.

Isvaran's stories cannot be considered mere description of events or delineation of a situation. The event or situation in some way illumines the lives of the readers. This is achieved by shaping the events in such a way as to extract a meaning out of it. Isvaran seems to follow the principle of the modern short story, "they either add to our knowledge of life or else give us a fresh or subtly qualified or vividly dramatized idea."[24] Traditionally the story has been considered the body and the moral its soul.

Some of the stories of Isvaran are modelled on the traditional fable in which he uses a conception purely fantastic and somewhat trivial to convey a moral precept. For example, in the stories, "Bewitched," "A Bold Stroke" and "Thoughtless Donkey," the essential elements of the story are playfulness and concision and the moral lesson is apprehended by the fancy at half a hint. These stories bear the palpable unreality and moral simplicity of the primitive sort of fables of which Isvaran seems nostalgic.

The tone of Isvaran's stories is moral and didactic. Whether the matrix of the story is traditional or modern the didactic element predominates. The stories in the collection *Fancy Tales* are set in a world of magic and enchantment.

The analysis undertaken in the following pages bears out the truth of the contention that a theme-based classification of Isvaran's short stories often defies critical skill. Pigeon-holing of literary creations in general can be done only at the expense of clearly defined discriminative criteria. It is more so in the case of Isvaran's stories which have as their themes an extensive array of religious, ritualistic, social, familial, fantastic and fabulous features that seldom show any aversion to mingling among themselves. Nevertheless, an attempt is made to classify Isvaran's short stories thematically in broad, general terms, for the sake of convenience of critical analysis.

NOTES

1. *The Short Story: An Introduction* (New York: McGraw Hill, 1976), p. 23.
2. Lynn Altenbernd and Leslie L. Lewis, *A Handbook for the Study of Fiction* (London: Macmillan, 1966), p. 78.
3. *Loc. cit.*
4. Harry Shaw and Douglas Beiment, *Reading the Short Story* (New York: Harper, 1941), p. 13.
5. *A Handbook for the Study of Fiction*, p. 79.
6. Robert Gorham Davis, ed., *Ten Modern Masters: An Anthology of the Short Story*, p. 550.
7. *The Scope of Fiction* (New York: Appleton Crafts Division of Meredith Corporation, 1960), p. 229.
8. *Indian Short Story in English*, p. 33.
9. "Book Review," *Swatantra*, 9 April 1955, p. 33.
10. "The Stories of Manjeri Isvaran," *Thought*, 10 Aug. 1963, p. 12.
11. *Indo-Anglian Fiction: An Assessment* (Bareilly: Prakash, 1968), p. 9.
12. *Twice Born Fiction: Themes and Techniques of the Indian Novel in English* (New Delhi: Arnold Heinemann, 1971), p. 60.
13. *Swatantra*, 9 Sept. 1953, p. 30.
14. *Twice Born Fiction*, p. 26.
15. *Ibid.*, p. 34.
16. *Ibid.*, p. 30.
17. Preface to *A Madras Admiral*, p. 10.
18. *Indian Short Story in English*, p. 38.
19. *Angry Dust* (Madras: Suktikaryalayam, 1944), p. 3.
20. Isvaran, *Naked Shingles* (Madras: Chitrabhanu, 1941), p. 58.
21. *Angry Dust*, p. 47.
22. "The Stories of Manjeri Isvaran," p. 12.
23. *Indian Short Story in English*, p. 34.
24. *A Handbook for the Study of Fiction*, p. 79.

Stories: Political and Socio-Cultural

While the major concern of the contemporaries of Isvaran is to transform the changing realities of life into artistic form, Isvaran deals with a wide range of themes. The story "Between Two Flags," which deals with the national struggle for freedom and Gandhian movement, shows Isvaran's deep awareness of the contemporary social and political problems.

The story belongs to that class of fiction that manifests protest against the establishment. The story reveals Isvaran's capacity for the skilful use of art for propaganda. True to the spirit of a freedom fighter the nationalistic feelings culminate in a pronounced hostility to the British in this story. But it is clear that anti-British bias is not actually deep-rooted in Isvaran. His high moral standards in art as well as in personal life do not allow him to hate the British as individuals. He may be said to have imbibed the Gandhian ideals more in his personal life than in his literary creations.

"Between Two Flags" is the story of the son of a loyal bureaucrat who feels the pulls of the nationalistic forces. Rao Bahadur R. Kalyana Rao Sastri, Deputy Collector, "on the wrong side of sixty,"[1] is a man of no serious political leanings. If he has any, it has derived "its particular hue from loyal service." (52) For his meritorious service he gets promotions one after the other and the King's Birthday Honours bring him the title of Rao Saheb. Meanwhile, the freedom movement is gathering momentum. Rajaraman, the eldest son of Sastry, sixteen now, is a student in the sixth form. He is "immersed in his lessons" and "cheerful in his games." But the headmaster of the school feels that Rajaraman "should not allow certain ideas to get into his young heart." (58) Rajaraman feels otherwise and tells the headmaster outright that it is an insult to our motherland and a violation of self-respect to salute the Union Jack when our national leaders are being tortured and imprisoned by the white men. His declaration that he would salute the national flag of his country, and not that of the British, infuriates his father who slaps him on the cheek. For a few moments he stands stunned in disbelief, but soon recovers himself, and in a moment of irrational anger he destroys "the British gods" whom his father has enthroned within their home. Rao Bahadur "never forgave his son."

(63) He continues the life of a bureaucrat, till he finally retires from service as Deputy Collector. India, Isvaran notes, has turned out a "generation of Rajaramans, courageous, upright, selfless youths who, working under the inspiring guidance of heroic leaders courted a sacrifice as too great for the cause of the motherland." (64) Sastri does not know whether his son is alive or not.

The story is distinct from the other stories of Isvaran in the sense that, within the limited scope of a short story he gives ample opportunity to his characters to establish their identity as social beings by making them involved in the values and experiences which were valid in the Indian context of the pre-Independence period.

Isvaran had the primary source material for many of his short stories in the south India of the mid-decades of the present century, out of which he created a world of his own, varied and complete, as the original one. He had in mind a world dominated by British imperialism and bureaucracy but the background of his short stories was essentially that of the middle class or lower class. His social views and outlook on life reflect the limitations and contradictions of the class he has portrayed in his short stories. They cannot be separated from the social milieu in which he gained his own experiences. His genius is marked by a firmer grasp of the social conditions of the time and a deeper understanding of human nature. The picture of the countryside steeped in ignorance, illiteracy, superstition, inertia, petty jealousy, hatred and pride has been drawn with the insight of a philosopher and the empathy of a humanist, and without any attempt at idealization.

Isvaran was acutely conscious of, and indignant at, the social squalor, stagnation, wretchedness and poverty that he saw around him. He was intolerant of social repression, injustice and callousness, but his creative stance does not involve any criticism of a social or moral order. He gives a realistic picture of what he has seen and leaves it to the readers to formulate themselves the right reaction. It seems that his attitude to social problems was that of a liberal democrat. He has sympathy and love for all forms of life. His stories reveal that any social change to be enduringly effective must spring from a change of heart. His unhappiness with contemporary social conditions does not make him conceive a radical social change, but a gradual reformist change, an unhurried adaptation in which tradition and modernity go hand in hand, slowly emerging as a harmonious blend of both. His respect for tradition and his regard for the spirit of the modern age with its scientific outlook, coupled with the poise and dignity of his mind and personality impart a tone of authenticity to his liberal and evolutionary social philosophy.

With a more than perfunctory knowledge of the psychological and social life of the fisher folk on the Madras coast, Isvaran gives a revealing glimpse of their rugged and pitiless life in the story "Naked Shingles." The story gives an insight into their life "which hides a lot of pettiness and jealousy beneath the deceptive facade of rustic simplicity."[2]

Kali the good fisherman cherished a deep affection for his younger brother Mari. Kali's wife, Andayi, was an "exemplary housewife and shrewd business woman" who "sold well and to advantage" in the fish-market. Their "prosperity was matter for the envy of other garrulous fisher women."[3]

The trouble starts with Kali's lucky catch which is sold by Andayi for five rupees, a huge amount by contemporary standards. This provokes the enmity of Karuppayi, the wife of Vallathan, "the most noisy fellow in the Kuppam." (98) Karuppayi's "jealousy towards Kali's family was a smouldering fire which only needed a scandal concerning her to fan it into a leaping flame." (101) At first Vallathan tries to blackmail pregnant Andayi by linking her name with that of the unmarried Mari. Kali felt "wantonly insulted and was grieved beyond measure." (104)

Vallathan works on his evil designs. When they are in mid-sea on a stormy day, Vallathan feigns friendship with Kali and finishes him off with a huge boulder. Nothing remains but the memory of Kali cherished by Mari and Karuppayi in the posthumous child. The heinous crime enacted on the placid bosom of mother sea, which grants sustenance to, and fosters companionship among, the fisher folk, unravels to the reader the hidden dens of the human psyche that defy definition, explanation or classification.

"Mango Lane" is "the stimulating drama of feminine jealousy, rancour, conflict, defeat and finally compromise and co-existence."[4] It is the funny story of an 'appam' vendor meeting with retribution at the hands of mischievous fate as a result of her own evil contrivances on a rival in the same trade as hers. It is the hilarious tale of a feud between Kathayi—a "substantial black barrel of woman"[5] who "set herself up as an appam seller in the alley" (58) and her rival Tamarayi "a young woman not yet twenty." Tamarai not only triumphs but routs Kathayi utterly by marrying her son Chinnan. "God's ways are mysterious," (76) chuckles the author.

"Crutches" is, indeed, a gem of a short story in its deep pathos of true penitence chastening a girl's heart which in the grasp of jealousy against another of her own age had sought earlier to cause harm to her."[6] Srimati, the young wife of Panchanadan, engineered an accident which made her beautiful cousin Lalitha lame for life. Lalitha's loveliness was an eyesore to Srimati. "In a moment of blind jealousy" (53) she managed to slip an orange peel which caused her fall down and injure her leg which ultimately made her a cripple for the rest of her life. This incident ultimately mars the peace of mind of Srimati despite her attainment of what she expected to make her life happy.

The situation presented in the story "The Last Pawn" may be predictable and stale, but in the forties of the present century the themes of the exploitation of the poor by the heartless landlords and moneylenders attracted literary treatment by poets and novelists, especially of the regional languages. This is one of the 'proletarian' stories of Isvaran. The story reveals Isvaran's sympathy for the weaker sections of society.

It is the story of a poor mother pawning her ear-rings for a paltry sum to save her seriously sick child. The story begins with the description of a typical, pot-bellied Marwari moneylender, who is traditionally a merciless exploiter. His "clients were mostly of the weaker sex."[7] At the very sight of a woman swiftly approaching him, he could guess the purpose of her visit and how desperate she was. The poor woman of the story is the wife of a road-mender who is lying disabled for life in a little thatched hut outside the hem of the town. She is in a desperate situation, in her endeavours to save the life of "the only child left out of seven." (32) The moneylender offers to give two rupees for the ear-rings which, according to him, are a pair of "cheapstoned, colourless, common ear ornaments." (31) She makes in vain "a last attempt to beg for more." (31) The sole being of the woman turns out to be a "scintillating cell of pain." (33) She snatches the money and hurries away as Rickabdas Fathermal, the 'shylock' caresses his capacious belly. "The vision of the next auction sale floated like a veil before him." (34)

The fat doctor too is callous. He would not treat the child without 'proper' payment. In the evening of the same day the child dies. Though the story is a nightly sentimental tear-jerker seasoned with melodrama, it is a pointer to the filth and squalor of the society of the time.

In "Painted Tigers," Isvaran vividly describes the incident of a crime committed more by impulse than by pre-determination. Rivalry between two contestants at a tiger-masked display of muscular strength ends in a somewhat melodramatic collapse, as all of a sudden one of the two hears the news of the death of a one-time sweetheart of his. It is the story of a lover's revenge. Karim loves Ayesha. But she is forced to marry Umar and later happens to die because of the cruelty of the husband towards her. Karim gets his chance of revenge when both he and Umar are dressed up as tigers during the festival. They in their frenzy change from the fake to the real and in a maniacal fit one kills the other.

"Rickshawallah," the title story of the collection published in April 1946, is a proletarian story in the Gorkian mould. Like the stories of Chekhov who is always concerned with the themes of personal defeats and painful adjustments with unfriendly circumstances, this long short story portrays with sympathy, the struggle of a village-bred youth to come to terms with the unfamiliar urban circumstances where he finds himself as a result of a thoughtless act.

The story is a testimony to Isvaran's deep awareness of, and his preoccupation with, the element of accident and chance in human fate—a force acting independently and capriciously outside human will. Everything that happens in nature of which human life is an integral part has a causative factor which is often beyond human understanding. Man's deeds, good or evil, bear responsibility for his future. The Rickshawallah seems to be aware of this, after the death of a 'fare' for which he is held responsible. He knows that the major characters of the story, including himself, maintain sincere feelings and mutual goodwill, but his life remains tragic not because of the presence of any adversary but because of the circumstances which lie beyond the influence of the characters.

A village boy leaves behind his loving mother, his elder brother of high rural ambitions, and his house, and goes to the city never to return. "In the city all was not as he had expected, as he had dreamed."[8] His self-respect does not allow him to go back. "He could not decide upon a job that would suit him." (2) The little money he has with him is sufficient only for a few days. He becomes a rickshaw-puller, "to be away from the filthy pavements, from the ragged sickly beggars." (3) Within a short period he becomes a popular figure in the rickshaw-stand, "popular alike with the fares for his smartness and just demand." (4) He hopes to save enough to help his brother and fulfill his desires. One evening he becomes responsible for the death of a fare. The rickshawallah who is not a congenital criminal is remanded in custody for six weeks. The autopsy on the gentleman he "murdered" had revealed that the deceased had long been suffering from an enlarged liver. That was a circumstance favourable to him, that might mitigate the severity of his sentence. "He had not killed in wantonness . . . he had struck under grave provocation and in self-defence, the railway porter had testified to that effect." (10) On hearing the sad plight of the boy his family comes to see him in prison. "He could not stand the sight of his poor sobbing mother, could not bear the caressing touch of her." (11)

While the Rickshawallah is in prison, his mother dies. When he is released, his brother waits eagerly near the gates of the prison yard to take him back to the village. But he will not darken their "threshold by his sinful presence." In the city he will be just be "a drop in the ocean."

The Rickshawallah resumes the work in the same stand with the same rickshaw which has been kept intact by its owner Mastan Khan, for the same rent. There is no significant change in the premises. Nobody talks about his crime. He tries in vain to be as cheerful as he was before. The shadow cast on him by the tragic incident makes him grow more and more inward. This in turn causes a deterioration of his physical health and "in his entombed hours he seemed a sculptured sorrow, commemorative of his own self-immolation." (25)

The Rickshawallah becomes more pious, and offers prayers in a way befitting his condition. He visits shrines as a routine. He resists the advances of the daughter of the woman who brings the rickshawallahs of the stand, their noon meal. He always feels lonely among the crowd.

The Rickshawallah's physical condition gradually worsens. On a Thursday, he is in constant demand all through the day. It is a day on which he has unusually large earnings. He is much in need of rest. He is on the brink of a break-down, when a middle-aged woman and her little child ask him to drop them at the station. They have to catch the 8.30 train. After taking them safely to the station, the Rickshawallah falls down dead.

Isvaran, like Tolstoy, feels that human nature cannot be changed fundamentally. What Tolstoy conceives as both necessary and possible is a change of heart. What the Rickshawallah undergoes, especially after the prison life is such a change. Even his indifference to the feminine charms of the girl who tries to marry him is a part of it. Moralization gets the better of art in this story.

"Strictly Professional" narrates with wit and irony the indifference and callousness of a nurse towards the patients in her care. This is revealed by her talk with a fellow passenger, which the author overhears while he is travelling in a town bus.

"Counsel for the Defence" is a neatly constructed story which exposes the cunning and intrigue, so much a part of the Indian way of life, especially that of the south India of Isvaran's days. Such disputes as dealt with in the story arise out of the peculiarities of the social structure. The story is sinister in many of its aspects. It is narrated by a friend of the author who is a reputed lawyer. Two women lay claim to a new-born infant as being its mother. The two versions of the story and the truth unravelled to him finally reveal that "the man who bargained was as blind as a bat to the most noble and natural of all human feelings."[9]

The narrator of "That Moan" is an alter ego of the author himself and the 'wife' in the story is a good study of feminine psychology."[10] One cold December night, the narrator lies awake in his bed, when he hears the moan of a woman in the nearby street. Then it resolves into an "abrupt shriek," "sharp like a stab." He wakes up his wife but is not courageous enough to go out. The next morning he learns "some woman has given birth to a child and thrown it in the dust bin."[11] What is more significant than the gruesome episode is the reaction of the narrator's wife.

The stories concerned with contemporary social reality, a graphic delineation of actual life related to the individual self or the locale of the author form a significant group. In these stories the events and characters are drawn exactly as they were in the world familiar to Isvaran. His response to all that he observes is coloured with his characteristic warmth and intensity of feeling. Certain characters and objects set his mind in a state of dream or fantasy which crystallizes into fine tales. The actual facts observed suggest the story and create the specific mood, feeling and atmosphere. "Angry Dust" is a story of this kind. In a talk that Isvaran broadcast on the All India Radio, New Delhi on November 9, 1964, entitled "I came to Delhi" in the series "The First Time," he recollects his experience: "I spent doleful evenings under the auspices of the ghosts of the Moghul Emperors. Here was ancient dust redolent of royal blood. I climbed the Qutub which reared its head like a sultan's dream. I yearned to roam the desert palaces of Shajahan but could not, as it was wartime."[12] Towards the end of the talk he observes:

> I was sitting in my favourite spot, lost in a reverie, presently, a lorry-load of khaki-clad sons of the land of the five rivers, stalwarts all, with gleaming bayonets fixed to their guns dashed past me, perhaps bound for the Middle East. Hardly a mile away stood the Vicegral Lodge, on a rising eminence, in the splendour and loneliness of its isolation. The imperial flag fluttered in the wind as if the British lion roared in agony.

The picturesque sights leave the poetic mind of Isvaran in a reverie on the glory of the Moghul past, the sad plight of the descendants of the Moghuls and the pride of the Vicegral rule and the contemporary crisis of the British empire. The experiences of this reverie emerge in the story "The Angry Dust" which mingles facts with fantasy.

"Gold on His Lips" is apparently the story of a mad woman, but it draws the unforgettably vivid picture of a bazaar scene of Malabar, with which the author was quite familiar in his youth. In the story the narrator can be identified with the author, for a substantial portion of the story is devoted to the recollections of the narrator's childhood memories of the place and its people. Isvaran here refers to real places and people and experiences. More significant is Isvaran's answer through the story to the question, "Where does a writer get his ideas from?" (39) Commenting on the collection of short stories, *Painted Tigers*, K.R. Srinivasa Iyengar writes: "They turn on a wayward mood, a speck of experience, or a recovered spasm of memory. 'A true author,' Shri Isvaran confesses, 'bases his stuff on the facts of his own experience, while one is not true, on those of other writers.' Shri Isvaran's is always authentic writing for it is the expression of authentic experience."[13] The objective world presented here is convincingly real. The events and characters are exactly as they are believed to be in the actual world. The people and places in these stories can be identified with those in certain places near Calicut. At the same time the story is marked by the strong feelings of the author that the essential reality of things is created by what people feel about them. In an article entitled "Two Creative Artists," Isvaran writes:

> Away from Malabar for over two decades and a half—except for three or four hurried visits—and settled again in Tamil Nad, my parent country, my heart was filled with nostalgia for my foster-land. Mention of the poet quickened boyhood memories. I sank into a reverie-nostalgia and the smooth rolling of the roadster abetting. I was listening to the lines of Laurence Hope, the ill-starred English poetess Adela Florence Nicholson (divested of her pseudonym) who died by her own hand, of poisoning, and lies buried in St. Mary's Cemetery, Madras. They are about a man of Malabar returning after his wanderings, "from beneath the cruel stars of the frozen North," whose joy at the sight of his native land is thus given expression to:
>
> These are my people, and this my land.
> I hear the pulse of her secret soul,
> This is the life that I understand. . . .
> Oh, palm-leaf thatch, where the melon thrives,
> Beneath the shade of the tamarind tree,
> Though coverest tranquil, graceful lives,
> That want so little, they know no haste,
> Nor the bitter goad of a too-full hour,
> Where soft-eyed women are lithe and tall,
> And wear no garment below the knee,
> No veil or raiment above the waist,
> But the beautiful hair, that dowers them well,
> And falls to the ground in a scented shower.[14]

This passage and the poem appear in the story with some alteration. The story depicts the miseries of a young woman who runs mad as a result of being jilted by a faithless lover. Part of the story consists of her own narration, of the poignant story of the deception by her lover. K. Chandrasekharan considers the story "yet another pointer to the society to cure itself of callousness in the face of wrong and inhumanity."[15]

"Posthumous Award" is the story of a soldier who is given "the highest and most coveted distinction of every soldier," the Victoria Cross posthumously for "the gallant services."[16] The irony of the situation is that the soldier, Subedar Ratnaswami, who is supposed to have been killed in action in Tripolitana, has really escaped death and is present at the ceremonious function wherein his wife Paanchali receives the award.

Ratnaswami who has miraculously escaped from the clutches of death reaches home. What he experiences there is beyond his endurance. He narrates his painful experience at home:

> I was a stranger in my own house! Denied by my mother, denied by my wife, and perhaps disowned by my father when he lay dying! What a welcome for a man from his nearest and dearest! Only a frozen unrecognition. What a welcome for a hero who had served his King and saved the Empire! Only a sepulchral silence. (110)

Ratnaswami is a silent witness to the "eventful" journey of his wife and mother to New Delhi to receive the award. He expects that they would seek some male help on the journey. But they do not. He notices "a curious remoteness and self-intentness in the two women, a dignity which they had suddenly become heir to." (111)

Ratnaswami follows them silently to New Delhi and attends the function and witnesses the placing of the "prize of illimitable glory, the Victoria Cross, in the hands of the widow of the late Subedar Ratnaswami." (112) As he is watching the proceedings, he catches the cry of his baby with a pang and catches, too the abrupt drone of bombers haunting the skies and saw villages after villages shattered and smoking, half-clad hysterical women and screaming children. (113) Ratnaswami who joins the army to earn a living for his family, experiences the thrill and horrors of war, comes away from Egypt to his native village after many hardships to console his mother and wife, is neglected by all at home and finally becomes a spectator at the grand function got up to honour him. His views on the meaninglessness of what he has experienced and what others consider supreme achievements echo in the following words of Ratnaswami:

> Award of the Victoria Cross to Subedar Ratnaswami for supreme valour beyond the call of duty! But what does it signify to my poor little wife? Ah, but you my child, you are favoured of the Gods for you are a female, and you will not have to enlist as a soldier, in the event of another World War. There's fulfilment in your being a girl, my darling, and no little bliss for me beyond the grave. (113)

"The War Memorial" is a story of parental love, a story in the conventional groove. It portrays the suffering and sorrow of aged parents at the death in the war of their only son, as they stand in front of the war memorial. Nureddin, the young tailor, twenty-three, had his shop in a quiet nook of the city. He finds it difficult to live on a "measly eight annas a day."[17] He is not even able to give a meal a day to his aged parents. So, despite the objections of his parents, he joins the army and is later killed in action at the Mesopotamian war front.

Nureddin's father, Gulam Ali, whose ancestors had once served the puissant Nawabs of Arcot, and mother Begum Resham Jan are consoled by the 'stately War Memorial' constructed to commemorate those who had fallen in the field of honour, for they could not build a tomb for him, light the light, and pray beside his tomb.

Thematically this tale has little in common with the other stories of Isvaran. Perhaps he intended to romanticize war by eulogizing the parents who felt a sort of pride in their son who had sacrificed himself at the altar of patriotism. Or, Isvaran may be talking with his tongue in his cheek when he presents the cryptic contrast between the inspiring words on the memorial ("fallen in the field of honour"[52]) and the real reason that inspired Nureddin to take up arms (the "measly eight annas a day" that he earned as a tailor).

"Peaceful was the Night" tries to distil the pity of war in a Wilfred Owenesque manner. Its similarity to the earlier story "Posthumous Award" is merely superficial. The death of the soldier in battle figures in both, but "the areas of experience explored in the two stories are fundamentally different."[18] Paul Tambidurai, Subedar Major, "had gone through a week of quick manoeuvres" and "many a familiar face was missing from their ranks."[19] Then "came a call before the final onslaught." (83) Tambidurai sits at the entrance of his bivouac. He falls into a reverie on Christmas. He has a vision of the magic and the newborn babe, Christ, in the manger with the mother bending over the baby. Soon the beatific vision is shattered by the drone of an enemy bomber. Horrors of war with its diabolic weapons sweep through his consciousness. He realizes that "a generation of men were destroying themselves in order, so they believed, to make the world safe for the next. But war begets war. And how with evil to cast out evil." (89)

The story "Decision" captures a facet of Indian life which has rarely been presented in Indian writing in English. The author sums up in the incidents of a night the significant experience of a lifetime. The story is remarkably poignant in its description of a woman of thirty, Sarada, who is deprived of motherhood even after ten years of her marriage with Janardanan. Miraculously she conceives after having seen a cow giving birth to a calf. The rapture of incredulity at the parturition on the part of the woman is described by Isvaran with a realism that any mother would accept with tears and gratitude.

The theme of "Tu Quoque" is the incorrigibility of a born thief Essakki who is convicted for stealing the necklace of a four-year-old girl. Incarceration for two years brings about a change in him, but the inborn tendency to steal remains. After having completed the term of imprisonment, he is taken to Madras escorted by a policeman. While travelling in the train he tries to appropriate for himself a currency note that has slipped out of the pocket of a sleeping passenger. When the hand of the policeman reaches the note first instead of his, he feels cheated of his due.

Isvaran deals dreams and nightmares in some of his stories. "The Man behind the Chair" is a sketch rather than a shapely modern short story. It deals with a nightmarish experience on the part of the author as well as "the man behind the chair," a barber, who narrates his long, eventful, poignant story to the author. At a certain stage in the story there is a sudden straight leap from the pathetic to the grotesque. He says, "and after the hospital I was in the asylum for four months."[20] On hearing this, the narrator notices "the queer glitter of his eyes. He was concentrating" (80) on the throat of the author who feels "a wild inclination to thrust him back and rush out." (81) After very anxious moments, "with a sigh of relief" the narrator sees the barber "laying aside the murderous razor." "Restless like a centipede in humid heat and putting a rupee in his hand," (81) the narrator darts out without even waiting for the balance of fourteen annas, for the barber's charge is only two annas. He feels like "one risen from a nightmare." (81)

The story "Toilette" forms a part of the reflection of the narrator on the episodes in the crowded third class compartment of Calcutta Mail in which he is also a passenger. The central character of the story, a young Andhra woman, who "looked like an Ajanta carving come to life,"[21] quite oblivious to her surroundings, does her hair and toilette. Her husband, a middle-aged man, who accompanies her, is indifferent to, and even ignorant of, her natural charms and youthful longings.

The story can be described as though it were a kind of verbal equivalent of an impressionist painting in which stress is on the physical surface like the tone, colour and texture. The total effect is created by the narrator's visual memory, and the exquisite rendering of his impressions of the world around him. His voice merges with the thoughts, the words and the very mode of perception of the central character. Isvaran's narrator provides here a substantial foreground, a general mood by means of a suggestion in the long introductory part of the tale and in the inset we have mere sketches of people he sees around him. In the most characteristic manner of Chekhov, Isvaran concentrates on details of appearance, and a brief touch of fantasy. Actually nothing "happens" in the story.

Unlike the other tales of Isvaran there is a total absence of didactic element in the "Toilette." The narrator's reflections and reactions are more significant than those of the central character, for the reader sees her through the eyes of the narrator. As far as the narrator is concerned, "every little reflection freshens and vitalizes the mind," (36) an experience which he transmits to the readers.

The stories "Annihilation" and "Only a Sparrow" are inspired by real experiences. In an informal talk, Mr. K. Venkataraman, Isvaran's brother-in-law and a very close associate, revealed that seemingly insignificant things like the death of a sparrow or the cutting down of a lemon tree exercised a deep and abiding imprint on Isvaran's sensitive mind. "Only a Sparrow" is a simple account of the great compassion a man might feel for a dying bird. It is one of "the many stories of Isvaran presenting animals in human light."[22] "Annihilation" expresses the deep sorrow of the author at the cutting down of a lime tree in the compound of Isvaran's neighbour. Both the stories are little more than sketches. The stories analyzed in the chapter are seen to be poetic visions and memories of observed life transformed into something new and beautiful by the creative mind of Isvaran. Sensitivity and delicacy, nimbleness and introspection characterize the author's approach to life as revealed in these stories.

NOTES

1. *No Ankletbells for Her* (Madras: Mitra, 1949), p. 52.
2. D. Anjaneyulu, "Stories of Manjeri Isvaran," *Thought*, 10 August 1963, p. 12.
3. *Naked Shingles* (Madras: Chitrabhanu, 1941), p. 93.
4. "The Stories of Manjeri Isvaran," p. 13.
5. *Painted Tigers* (Madras: Dhanus, 1956), p. 56.

6. K. Chandrasekharan, "Manjeri Isvaran's Stories," *The Hindu*, 29 January 1959, n.p.
7. *Angry Dust* (Madras: Shakti Karyalayan), 1944, p. 29.
8. *Rickshawallah* (Madras: Alliance, 1946), p. 2.
9. *No Ankletbells for Her*, p. 48.
10. K. Ayyappa Paniker, *Manjeri S. Isvaran*, Kerala Writers in English Series, 1, V.1.5 (Madras: Macmillan India, 1983), p. 44.
11. *Painted Tigers*, p. 108.
12. Ts, Isvaran's personal library, New Delhi.
13. Rev. of *Painted Tigers, The Aryan Path*, Nov. 1956, p. 521.
14. Ts, Isvaran's personal library, New Delhi.
15. "Manjeri Isvaran's Stories," n.p.
16. *Rickshawallah*, p. 112.
17. *Naked Shingles*, p. 47.
18. Paniker, p. 37.
19. *No Ankletbells for Her*, p. 83.
20. *Angry Dust*, p. 79.
21. *Rickshawallah*, p. 40.
22. Paniker, p. 44.

Stories: Familial

Isvaran's genius is marked by a deeper understanding of the nature of his men and women in their different relationships in the family as well as in society. His portrayal of the narrow and circumscribed life of the middle class with accuracy and imaginative vision shows how intimate his knowledge is of the life of his people in their varied moods and turns. Isvaran's art is manifest in his most characteristic stories, in finding "the mind's construction" in human responses and reactions in a variety of situations.

In "Mythili" Isvaran presents a sensitive young husband involved in a humiliating situation and his immediate reaction to the situation and a final realization of his folly. A young householder, an N.G.O., "whose salary starts on a benevolent minimum of thirty rupees a month"[1] is moving house. He consulted the almanac and found out an auspicious date for moving to the new premises. "A handcart was to do two trips, the first of which was to carry my shelf-ful of books, sundry wooden furniture and clothes boxes to be preceded by my wife and child in a rickshaw." (38) The young N.G.O. is to precede the second trip. He doesn't know what things he has piled up in the cart, "in the hurry and excitement of the migration." (38) On the way he notices people snickering at his possessions like "the blackened oven of baked clay gaping like a gargoyle, a couple of brooms sticking out of its mouth, near it a loosening bundle of split firewood entangled in a clothes-line, the pole to dust off cobwebs trailing its dishevelled beard." (39) He goes "pale with anger, purple with shame." He rushes ahead leaving the cartman "to follow in his own good time." (40) The irate husband, put to shame by the public exposure of his poverty, for which he alone is responsible, unjustly vents his frustration on his wife Mythili. He soon realizes the injustice of his enormous outburst. Mythili, a typical Hindu wife, a symbol of love and tolerance, who values domestic harmony and welfare, forgives him readily. He says, "Mythili has never asked me why I burst like mad upon her on the day we moved house. Thank god, she is not the capable sort; her understanding is riches to me." (48) The change in the husband's mood, from blind fury to repentance and love—and an enactment of an exciting human drama of shifting reactions has been presented in about a dozen lines.

"Revelation" is a story of high artistic order. A remarkable concentration of material, an amazing insight into the mind of the young couple, a dramatic presentation of theme, the exciting quality of the dialogue and narration, all make the story an outstanding piece. The atmosphere that informs a traditional orthodox Brahmin family, the picture of a mother-in-law in such a family, the psychological state of the young husband and wife on various occasions in their domestic life have all been presented in this story with remarkable insight.

"Brihadisvaran and Savitri had been married two years."[2] (Originally Isvaran was named Brihadisvaran.) Their marriage "was solemnized in the ancient orthodox way." (25) The story begins with an indication of the state of mind of Savitri on the third anniversary of their nuptial night. The hilarity and eloquence of beautiful Savitri, who is an ideal wife, is primarily on account of the temporary freedom she enjoys on account of the absence of the mother-in-law who is away for a fortnight in her daughter's house. She chooses this occasion for the revelation of the long cherished secret. Brihadisvaran who is mystified at the unusual joviality of his young wife asks her why she is so excited.

For the past two years Brihadisvaran has been under the impression that the young bride on the first night was sleeping soundly as he was walking up and down the terrace for hours in an agony of indecision, quite characteristic of a newly wedded youngman. Finally he entered the room mustering up enough courage to approach the young bride. He thought that the bride was fast asleep. However, everything ended well. The wife now reveals the secret to him. She says "I kept my head on the pillows in such a manner as to cover part of your pillow also. When you finally entered the room, I feigned deep sleep and watched you all the while through half-closed lids." (29)

"Saturday is Saturday" is a picture of the romantic longings and youthful desires of a young couple who have been married for three years, she at seventeen and he at twenty-four. The young wife is in her parental home. Now the husband is coming back from Bombay after the first long separation in their married life. She gets the thrill of her life in reading her husband's letter announcing his arrival "on Saturday by Bombay Express."[3] She makes elaborate preparation to appear at her best to receive him. "She caught herself glancing at the mirror every now and again, wistfully, provocatively; she winked at her image pulling out a lock here, patting down a lock there. She smiled, her reflection smiled." (127) As she is busy with her preparations he comes on Friday, a day earlier than scheduled. The story is an amazingly minute study that captures the elusive charm of conjugal relations in a typical middle class family of the south.

In contrast to the familial atmosphere presented in the story "Revelation," Isvaran presents in the long story "Consummation" the state of mind of an ultra sensitive husband, who becomes cynical as a result of the premature death of his wife that shatters thereby the peace of the entire home.

The theme of "A Light was Lit" is sisterly and brotherly feelings, with a deep insight into the intricate workings of the human mind. Isvaran leads the reader of the story to a recognition that the underside of all human experience, even the most mundane has its mysteriously tragic aspects which others cannot understand. The setting for the story is provided by the 'Kartika festival' at which lamps are lit in Hindu houses. "It's the day when women light lamps and pray . . . for the well being and long life of their brothers. It is an occasion exclusive to brothers and sisters." (116) Parvati is distraught on this occasion because the day reminds her of her brother who absconded five years ago. Her mother-in-law who notices the sad Parvati is not however sympathetic. She blames her for being so sad on such an auspicious day.

"Passage Money" presents certain interesting episodes, the end of which exhibits the embarrassing plight of a father who is rudely made aware of the fact that his daughter Kumudam has attained womanhood which he has completely failed to notice. The story describes the prolonged and fidgety waiting that the passengers do to catch a bus, the whims and fancies of the conductor "with something distinctive of the mongrel in his appearance."[4] The mental state of the wife caused by the ignorance of her husband about their daughter's attainment of womanhood, the exchange of hot words between the conductor and the head of the family, the shock caused by the news about his daughter, and finally the payment of full fare for Kumudam which enables them to continue the journey.

The theme of the story "Overwrought" is the sense of isolation and hopelessness experienced by a young wife caused by the indifference of her husband and the overpowering presence of a domineering mother-in-law. The tragic story of the nineteen-year-old Padma is woven round the basic emotions of love, jealousy and despair. The story begins with suggestions of the familial disharmony caused by the jealousy and lack of proper understanding. At the very instance of seeing Padma, her mother-in-law's face becomes clouded and her lips curl in contempt. The response of the husband Jambu to her light, loving touch is eloquent: "He looked at her aslant and frowned, the hebdomadal growth on his face bristling like quills upon the fretful porpentine."[5] Jambu suffers from frayed nerves on account of heavy work as clerk to an exacting barrister and abnormal attachment to his mother who is in her late forties and who still dominates the whole family. Padma bursts out: "It is mother, mother, mother always. Then what am I here for? What is a wife for?" (15) Things become worse with the arrival of Lalita, Jambu's cousin, to stay for a few days. Lalita is beautiful. She was once destined to be married to Jambu. The sense of alienation and jealousy created by the intimacy among Lalita, Jambu and the mother-in-law goads Padma on to commit suicide: "it was with her sari that the jealous, overwrought girl had tied the fatal knot." (27)

"Stepmotherhood has a tradition as old as the epics, and Irulayi hadn't the heart to tarnish its glory." (46) The story, "No Birds Sing" is the tragic tale of domestic cruelty, disintegrating an entire family, all caused by the malevolence of a stepmother. Varian "had tied the tail round Irulayi's neck only because of an ardent desire, of a sense almost of sacred duty, to give his children a loving mother, a kindly soul to care for them, to protect them." (46-47) No child was born to her even after the expiry of twelve years. The embittered Irulayi with her "yearning feminity which was starved, rebelled against the unmaleness of her man in mingled contempt and disgust, and hated his children whom it regarded as imps mocking her sterility." (47) For this she continually persecutes the children, Chengalani who is employed in an aluminium factory and Valli who helps her in the domestic chores. "But the sight of her tyranny over his darlings sickened his heart." (48)

The boy dies of a road accident and his sister Valli, who could not bear the sight of "the mangled remains of all that was her brother," (58) commits suicide by jumping into the temple tank. The heart-broken Varian goes mad and wanders about the streets of the city.

Irulayi is sentenced to imprisonment for six months by the Presidency Magistrate, Egmore, for running a brothel. "Before she had done half her time in the Vellore Jail she was transferred to the asylum in Kilpauk. The dead were avenged." (61)

"Heart of Man" is the story of an egocentric and unhappy man and his epileptic wife, revealed through a series of letters which the narrator receives during a period of a decade and a half. The narrator maintains:

> As in water face answereth face
> So the heart of man to man.[6]

II

The theme of many stories of Isvaran is the misery of women caused knowingly or unknowingly by men. In the male scheme of things, man, it seems, is supreme, immune to moral pressures, or thoughts of familial obligations. A woman on the contrary is not so conditioned. In the world of the family she occupies only a secondary position, the pride of place always willingly and even happily yielded to the husband or (in his absence) to the son. Seldom is she the shaper of her own destiny: it is inextricably entangled with the whims and fancies of her husband or her son as the case may be. Indian legends teem with such characters. 'Seelavathi' is their model.

The story "Merry Go Round" with which the volume *Naked Shingles* opens is the portrayal of a poignant human situation in colourful phrasing and imagery. It is the touching tale of Ratnam given to drinking and betting on horses and his wife Mangi "a cubistic female, all harsh lines and no flesh." (13) More than her husband's death what shocks and pains her is the words of her son on listening to the tale of his father's tragic death: "I too would bet." (15)

"The Motorman" is the story of Yellen, the 'motorman' who took a fancy to Vallachi, "a perfect she animal that raises the animal spirits in man." (59) Yellen's wife Gangi is a trusting and devoted girl. As a result of his infatuation, Yellen grows fretful and often "indifferent to the speed zones." (60) In spite of his "perfect control over the brakes," (60) he meets with an accident which causes the amputation of his leg. Even after that, "the rascal was hoping and hoping that Vallachi would come, come to see him, would come with orange." (61) But she does not come. He leaves the hospital, finally breaking himself free from delusions as he sees "a gleam of light" (62) which seems to illumine his virtuous and long suffering wife with a radiance he understood.

Though a major part of his story is set apart to present the delusion caused by sexual jealousy, the focus is on the masochist streak in the wife's mental make up. The Yellens of this world always get away with their escapades inflicting suffering on their wives. But their wives never rebel. They wait patiently, eternally hoping for the eventual return of their spouses. The wife's is a dubious triumph.

"Jowramma" is the story of a poor peasant, Mali, who leads a quiet, pleasant life with his wife Jowramma, "in her early twenties, small made, prettyish, full of that lush of muliebrity commonly found in hill-girls." (18) The quiet flow of their life is temporarily interrupted by the arrival of the Assistant Secretary and his family to live in their neighbourhood. The temptation that the town's folk proffer is so powerful that Jowramma decides to leave her husband on the farm and go to Madras with the Assistant Secretary's family. When she reaches the railway station to leave for Madras, she changes her mind, not because of any intelligent thinking or logical reasoning but because of her ardent though undemonstrable love for her husband. She returns to the farm to her husband. "In his tight clasp she felt the strength and silence of the hills and trees round, in the dew of her lips he tasted the sweet of life and the salt of the earth." (30)

The story movingly delineates some of the deepest moods and moments in the life of a simple rural belle. What makes her prefer, ultimately, the familial home? Psychologically she is tethered to an existence, the life and soul of which is her husband. She does not have the grit to break loose and lead a life of her own. She lives in a cell made by herself, for herself and her master, the husband. There is no escape from it, and she does not want to escape from it. She represents the typical Indian woman.

Syamala, the heroine of the story "Sea Shells," cannot visualize a life without her husband. Like the average run of Indian women, she considers her husband the only reason for leading a happy life.

In the story "Mythili" Isvaran presents a typical Hindu wife who values the welfare of her husband and domestic harmony more than anything else in life.

The agony of a widow's life is the major theme of "Sympathy." The focus in the story is on Anandalakshmi, a middle-aged woman of a typical middle-class Brahmin family, the mother of Gomathy who has become a widow soon after her marriage. She dresses and behaves like a widow. She does it to the amazement of her neighbours and the annoyance of her husband. Then one day violating the conventions of the orthodox Brahmins, Gomathy finds a husband for herself. Despite the pejoration of the social voice, Anandalakshmi is "happy in her daughter's happiness," and she cares "for nothing more, praise or blame, compliment or censure."[7] Though the husband is happy at the re-marriage of the widowed daughter and his wife's regaining normalcy, he is worried about his own sister who too is a widow!

III

In half a dozen stories Isvaran's protagonists are children presented in their multi-faceted relationships in the family and in society. These stories with their vivid descriptions reveal his intimate knowledge of child life in the families of the middle and lower classes. He probes into the working of their mind and lays bare their innocent longings.

In "No Ankletbells for Her," a little girl of nine or ten years finds "honest pleasure at her own smart appearance" in the "croup of the car" that "shone like cheval glass," (2-3) and dances spontaneously, unheeding the outraged screams of her mother. She "went on imitating steps, gesturing with fingers." (3) But her world of the ecstasy of art is suddenly shattered with the arrival of her scolding mother and the return of the owner of the car, a fashionably "dressed young lady, chic as a film star." (4) Annakili and her mother, characters drawn from lower classes, remain earth-bound and typical, resonate as they do the fanciful feelings of the vast human mass out of which they come. Their thoughts and deeds may appear wretched and tribal. But the author endows their commonplace world with a magnificence of its own.

"Kolu" is a story of the petty griefs and joys of children. Here grief is caused by a stepmother who is traditionally a symbol of hard-heartedness and discrimination. Sarasu, a motherless girl of eight, is a friend of Kamala living in the same street, four doors away. One day Sarasu steps into the house of Kamala with her younger brother and sister on invitation during the Kolu festival which has "a touch of heaven as well as of earth."[8] All the joys of the children on seeing the beautifully decorated dolls and at the taste of sweetmeat is shattered by the shriek of the stepmother outside the house. "Tears welled into the eyes of the two sisters while their little brother scattered his handful of peas in manly protest." (72)

"Beginnings," a brief story depicting the sparkling wonderland of childhood's make-believe games, is typical of "the poetry of laughter."[9] "Two girls, apparently of the same age—they might be five—bustled about animatedly whilst a boy, a year older, sat leaning on a pillar and watching them."[10] They play at house-keeping, roping in the boy as husband. On the issue of who is to be the wife, "the girls began to quarrel without further check, pecking at each other like birds, pulling the hair, clawing and snarling like vicious cats." (36) The poor "husband," unable to do anything, remains a passive spectator to whatever goes on before him. "Janaki had the worst of it . . . and she subsided into a fit of sobbing. At this Jagadisan came to her and throwing his arms round her neck" (36) consoled her. "Janaki smiled through her tears. . . . Girija stood like a demon, her bosom heaving" and she "kicked about the cooking utensils." (36) When Jagadisan and Janaki "walked out slowly, whispering together and glancing furtively once behind," Girija stood "lost in an abyss of forlornness. The golden home they were building had suddenly blanched lead." (37) The author here is looking at the children's world not through adult eyes or with any touch of condescending sympathy. He is back in his own childhood and records in all seriousness the 'mighty wars' and 'poignant tragedies' of that age. He is not a mere observer here, but a participant.

The story "Death of a Doll" is based on an actual incident. It is about an eight-year-old girl who dies in the hospital, of excessive burns. The narrator too is in the children's ward with his boy who has fractured his right arm. Despite the prayer of everyone who knows the girl, she dies leaving behind her "a doll fairly large sized" and beautiful.

In "Justice," Isvaran shows how the law of the land is against the poor. The story sets forth the significant events of a day in the life of a fourteen-year-old waif, a representative of countless waifs and beggars found in Indian cities and towns. The poverty of the boy sleeping on the plinth of the Rippon Statue in the morning is expressed in the following sentence: "His loin-cloth which was a piece of discarded gunny had fallen away; he seemed part of the beautiful black sculpture."[11] His day starts with the abuse of the Corporation servant who drives him out from the part with a kick on the buttocks. The scorching summer heat "entered the waif's stomach, and lay there like electric coils." (83) When hunger becomes unbearable he "begged the passers-by in the name of god for a pie, only a pie."[12] When he fails to get anything on the pavement he turns in vain to the restaurants. Then he snatches half a dozen plantains from a cart. He thrusts one greedily, skin and all, into his mouth but something like a vice round his neck holds him back from eating it. He is mute with misery. He is taken to the police station where he is charge-sheeted. The Magistrate sentences him to three years in the Borstal school. The author's unhappiness at the miserable plight of waifs and beggars like this has been eloquently expressed in the short authorial comment: "It was a triumph for the magistracies of the whole world." (86)

"A Gap in the Wall" tells the story of the casteless, classless world of children in which love and affection predominate, till their rosy dreams are shattered by the interference of the elders. Amrita, a rich man's daughter makes friends with Sokki "the girl from the cherry,"[13] "a low born stinking pariah dog!" (119) It is through a gap in the wall, created by heavy monsoon rain that they develop their friendship. The gap symbolizes "a loophole in the rigid class system that tried to segregate the classes."[14]

While the harijan girl enters the compound of the rich man through the gap to collect twigs, Amrita notices her and comes down to her. Soon they become friends, for Amrita had had few occasions to get acquainted with a girl of her age. Every day Sokki comes to collect twigs "accepting gracefully to eat whatever she expected for certain she would get. Such nice sweetmeats! such fine rice-cakes, so different from the appams which the women baked at the wayside of the cherry and sold two for an anna." (117) One day "the lady of the house had burst upon them and shattered their illusory little playworld." (118) Still they meet secretly every day. Days and weeks pass. People make hectic preparations for Deepavali. Amrita in "the accredited style of the ancient story-teller" (121) tells Sokki, how a certain demon was killed by God and why people celebrate Deepavali. Amrita promises to keep in the gap two packets containing sweets, a small bottle of oil for her bath and a pair of fine clothes. When Sokki's mother comes to know of this, she rushes to Amrita's house in wild fury, "dragging the half naked Sokki by her hair along the gravel drive." (124) She throws into the portico the contents of the packets and gives vent to all sorts of abusive words on Amrita. "By the evening of the next day hostile hands had filled the gap in the wall." (126)

In each of his stories dealing with child life, Isvaran depicts his characters in different social and familial relationships. Like Katherine Mansfield, Isvaran thinks himself inside each of his characters, thinking or speaking in their own voice. There is nothing mechanical about them. However, the limitation of the language he uses has little in common with the language used by children; it accounts for the credibility-gap in the juvenile tales of Isvaran.

NOTES

1. *Angry Dust*, p. 35.
2. *No Ankletbells for Her,* p. 25.
3. *Painted Tigers*.
4. *Rickshawallah*, p. 70.
5. *Angry Dust,* p. 14.
6. *No Ankletbells for Her*, p. 67.
7. *Ibid.*, p. 11.
8. *Naked Shingles,* p. 68.
9. D. Anjaneyulu, "The Stories of Manjeri Isvaran," p. 13.
10. *Naked Shingles,* p. 31.
11. *Angry Dust*, p. 82.
12. *Naked Shingles*, p. 83.
13. *Rickshawallah* p. 118.
14. Paniker, *Manjeri S. Isvaran*, p. 36.

Stories: Religious and Philosophical

Religion in India has always been a dominant force, exercising its hold on all spheres of human activity. This influence is manifest in the thoughts and actions of every Indian in his day-to-day life. Religion "consists of the inner development of the individual, the evolution of his consciousness in a certain direction which is considered good."[1] Isvaran, who was born in an orthodox family and brought up in the early years of his life in that custom-bound tradition, "tries to present the essence of the Hindu religious tradition, with all that is best in its myths and legends."[2]

Some of the stories of Isvaran are rich with Hindu philosophic thought. He fits philosophy into the plot in an admirably unobtrusive manner. The blend of religious philosophy endows his stories of the middle class with a charm that is not so evident in the stories which deal with other themes. Isvaran's fictional world is predominantly the Hindu world and naturally the religion that influences the lives and conduct of his characters is Hinduism.

Hinduism is not a religion with a corpus of doctrine, code of law or definitive scriptures. As William Walsh puts it: "It has its sacred, ancient, authoritative writings, the Veda and the later Epics, and in these works is implied a most distinctive, complex and inclusive vision of human life and destiny, which is neither messianic, progressive, triumphalist or millennial. As in the cluster of ideas which compose the notion of 'caste' there is a biological connection with purity and pollution, so in the Hindu conception of existence and destiny there is an organic parallel with creation and destruction. Existence is constituted by cycles of creation and decay. Just as in nature, forms and substances decay and are transformed into other forms and other substances, so the bodies and souls of man decay and are reborn in other modes of existence. The forces of creation and destruction are defined as Brahman, the creative power, and Shiva, the destructive power, which are not utterly opposed principles of a Manichean kind but are complementary aspects of Godhead, having their own echo or analogue in souls of men. There is no absolute distinction, we remember, between creator and creation in Hindu thought."[3]

Thus Hinduism is not a set of doctrines, it is a realization, a way of life, a potential spiritual force capable of remaking men. Central to its religious concepts is the soul, the divine spirit in man. The purpose of human life is the union of the soul with the divine by means of discipline and renunciation. The whole cosmic process in all its ascending stages from the mineral to the flora and the fauna, and from the natural man to the saints and the heroes, the avatars of humanity, is the manifestation of this divine spirit. Every individual soul operates in the divine process. So every birth is an incarnation. The soul survives the disintegration of the body and passes through a succession of lives till it is redeemed from the cycle of deaths and births and made one with the cosmic spirit: "The father, the head of the family, the mother in domestic life, the priestly caste—the Brahmins—in the conduct of ritual and the solution of ethical problems, the guru, the holy man, the ascetic who has renounced the world, the keeper of the temple, all have some of religious authority and work for the diffusion of Hindu values and the ordering of behaviour."[4]

Since the Vedic period, Hinduism has graded the social values on the basis of the inner spiritual progress which inevitably has led to a belief in plain living and high thinking. In this sense religious philosophy is something to be lived and not merely a mental gymnastic. Its application is to the essence of life, and the conduct of life.

The Hindu religious philosophy consists of the writings of the great masters right from the pre-Vedic period. Conflicting elements and widely divergent beliefs have evolved as a part of that philosophy. This apparently opposite faiths find a unity at certain levels. The Hindu concept of social organization is based on these divergent faiths. The basis of caste system can be attributed to this.

A man's state in a particular existence is determined by his actions in previous lives. His Karma in the present existence is a moral necessity. The idea of good and evil which ensures a better state of life in future existence is part of the belief of 'Karma' and accounts for the importance of ritualistic worship performed in temples and religious observances and ceremonies practised at home. These rituals are performed by Brahmins, for the welfare of the whole world. That is why Brahmins have enjoyed a pre-eminent position in Indian society. Time was when they alone had the privilege to acquire spiritual knowledge. They had an indispensable role to play in the performance of rituals in temples and religious observances, and on social occasions such as marriage, birth, death and 'upanayana.'

Religion, which thus forms an integral part of the social, cultural and familial life of the nation, cannot but be an integral part of the theme in Indian literature of which Indian writing in English forms an unignorable part. The attitudes to the multifarious aspects of religion vary widely depending upon the formative influences and temperament of each writer. Mulk Raj Anand is primarily preoccupied with the problems of untouchability and the evils of the caste system, economic exploitation and social injustice rampant in the Hindu society. He has handled these themes with a revolutionary zeal. He presents an Indian struggling forth on the road to political freedom, prosperity and modernity. As a man of the future, committed to science and Marxist humanism, he sees the past as a brutal drag on progress and enlightenment. Raja Rao has a profound sense of the richness and certainty of the past, metaphysical, poetic, traditional. Raja Rao and R.K. Narayan are deeply conscious and even proud of the rich cultural and religious heritage of the nation which they set forth in their works. They endorse and celebrate the traditional way of life and thinking.

The genesis of Isvaran's faculty of harmonizing the cultural and religious tradition with modernity in his short fiction can be traced back to the religious, cultural and social forces which influenced him by virtue of his birth in a Brahmin family of great antiquity as well as the culture of the modern West which he acquired by means of a Western system of education and contact with the West.

The upper middle-class Brahmin family in which he was born possessed a distinctive and individual tradition consisting of an amalgam of many elements, a way of life peculiar to Tamil Brahmins with all their religious observances and a deep and brooding self-introspection emanating from the inheritance as enjoined in the *Vedas* and the *Upanishads* and all that they signify. The routine life of the family in accordance with the stipulations of the scriptures in the early years of Isvaran, kept it apart from the mainstream of the national life.

While Tanjore, where he was born, was one of the seats of south Indian culture—temples, music and dances—and a fine blend of the Maratha tradition of sculpture and fine arts, Manjery where he spent his childhood and early youth was a small town in the Malabar district of the erstwhile Madras Presidency, the headquarters of the Ernad taluk, in the neighbourhood of Calicut, a city known for its cultural contact and commercial relationship with West Asian and European countries. The religious observances while he was in Manjery—the chanting of mantras from the scriptures, rituals associated with birth, marriage, death, temple ceremonies etc.—seem to have touched the sensibility of Isvaran deeply and abidingly and have later been instrumental in expanding the realm of his consciousness in an indefinable and intangible way.

Starting with the *Vedas* and the *Upanishads* he was in turn initiated in the study of Sanskrit classics. According to him, "the spirit that permeates the Upanishads, the Geetha and the immortal classics of the poets and playwrights of the ancient India"[5] has been there all through the ages giving rise to varied dimensions to the literature produced in the languages of India. The existence of a strong, conservative imagination particularly that of 'Hindu Samskara' formed and substantiated by a belief evolved from the collective experience of several generations prevails in many of the stories of Isvaran, especially those in which he depicts the life of his own class, the Brahmins, who in India have always enjoyed a prestigious position. Each member of this long line has considered it his duty to pay regular homage to the ancestors. So through the whole length of his life he has to observe a series of rituals which order his living. Prescriptions cover not religious rituals alone, but even dietary and sartorial tastes. Sacraments like rituals, sacrifices and prayers are spiritual experiences by means of which the life of a Hindu receives higher sanctity. These sacraments cover the entire life of an individual from the moment he is conceived in the womb of his mother till his death—inclusive of the funeral rites meant for the smooth transit of the soul to a world that promises freedom from any further incarnation.

The religious observances are primarily a means by which the individuals develop their moral virtues. They are ethical endeavours for the moral upliftment of the individuals. Every individual possesses a deep-rooted tendency to associate the chief events of his life with a higher power and to give his joys and sorrows a deeper significance and religious sanctification.

The earliest examples of these sacraments are found in the *Vedas*. The hymns and rules of marriage, conception, funeral, forms of worship, the initiation for Vedic studies are all found in them. The three major stories of Isvaran—"Immersion," "Sivaratri," and "The Dance of Siva"—are based entirely on spiritual and ritualistic experience.

The ceremonial immersion of the ashes of the protagonist's father is the pivot around which the plot of the story "Immersion" moves. The journey of Akhileswaran for the immersion of the ashes is "purely of a religious nature"[6] and an age-old practice. Akhileswaran thinks of his "father and his father's father before him who had travelled to Benares on a similar purpose." (22) It is the sacred duty of a son according to the cultural tradition of the protagonist—a racial belief and a social custom. It is something to be performed with great devotion and piety and so "Akhileswaran's thoughts hovered round the pot, thoughts of profound worship and devotion." (12) The protagonist was a "philosopher type, calm, meditative; he saw the city with a spiritual eye, as the centre of the

Hindu faith, soul illuminating, ever resplendent." (12)

The story owes much to the action of memory burdened with grief. The memory is predominantly ritual-based. Akhileswaran symbolizes the total acceptance of the traditional values of life. His memory is tinged with grief quite in keeping with the occasion. Here memory seems to make up the rhythm of life. The story begins with the onward journey in a bullock cart to the railway station and ends with the return journey in the same cart. Of the fourteen sections, the onward journey constitutes seven sections. Almost all sections are made up of the memories of the characters except those of the priest. Just before the loss of the pot, Akhileswaran recalls the occasion of his marriage with Jagada:

> the words of the Saptapadi echoing solemnly in his brain: "Seven steps have we taken together. Let us be companions. . . . Let me not swerve from fidelity to thee. . . . Swerve not thou from fidelity to me. . . . May our minds be in agreement, with the same resolves with the same thoughts. . . . I am the heaven. Thou art the earth. I am the seed. Thou art the receptacle. I am Mind. Thou art Speech. I am the Saman. Thou art the Rik."

A brooding haunting mysteriousness which invokes an atmosphere instinct with foreboding and a strange fear of something beyond one's sensory perception pervade the story. This in fact is the characteristic love for the simple and the mysterious of the traditional mind which Isvaran tries to unfold. This is not rational but intuitive. The timeless ideals inherent in the scriptures and puranas are brought forth along with their constituents such as symbolism, allegory, supernatural, rituals and archetypes.

The atmosphere of the story is replete with rituals associated with funeral and the subsequent rites; they make up the major reverie of the protagonist. The thing on which so much concern seemed to be concentrated was "an earthen pot fastened to the axle-tree of the cart." (12) The rituals have been accorded elaborate treatment in the story that begins with the thoughts of "the divine beauty" of his father's dead body "when it was washed and laid out," Akhileswaran reflects "he in his panchakachcha of immaculate white silk, with the sacred ashes and sandal paste adorning his forehead, the gold-encrusted rudraksha string lying gracefully round his neck . . . all his grandchildren had stood about him in a ring when he lay like that holding lighted flambeaus fed with ghee, strewing popped rice like milk-white flowers over the dead." (15) In the absence of the eldest son, Akhileswaran, who was temporarily away at his father-in-law's, "his younger brother had kindled the pyre." The pot containing the ashes lay buried "in the earth under a peepal that stood on the mound outside his house. The tree had been planted by his great grandparent . . . who had celebrated its upanayana and then married to a neem." (21)

> After six months during which Akhileswaran had devoutly performed his father's shraddha, the pot had been dug out from under the tree, and tonight, accompanied by his wife, he was travelling with it to Benares to consign it in the sacred waters of the Ganges. The auspicious day and hour for the immersion had been decided on by the family priest who had gone in advance of him to prepare and keep everything ready for the ceremony in the far-off holy city. (21)

The husband and wife who reached the holy city for the ceremony "had their preliminary lustral bath" (56) in the holy waters of the Ganges before the Immersion ceremony. The ceremony was performed amidst "the chants of the priests so sonorous and significant." (58) The tragic episode, the immersion of Jagadamma occurred when "the ceremony drew to a close." (59)

The Hindu faith associates tragic episodes with omens, portents, visitation of the souls of the dead and apparitions. The souls of the forefathers of Akhileswaran visit him just before the missing of the pot. "My son, you are betrayed!" sounded a voice apparently from the unknown. His brow wrinkled in perplexity. "Betrayed! It rang like a hammer on an anvil. It was the voice of his father. Unmistakably." (25) On the return journey the cartman sees the apparition of Jagadamma at a distance on the road:

> In the pale light of the cart lamp which obliterated the darkness for a few yards ahead, he saw the shadow of a figure which before he had seen it, the bullocks had, with the prescience common to animals, for they had become restive and as he gazed, all animation ebbing slowly out of him, up the yoke, along with the beam—a pair of glittering eyes, melancholy, wild, hair dishevelled and tumbling across its shoulders, its hands clenching, then a strangled cry like that of a wounded animal pierced the hollows of his ears, making his flesh crawl, tearing out the strings of his heart. (74)

Towards the end of the story Akhileswaran reflects: "The omens must have been bad when we set out for the journey." (47) According to the Hindu concept of life, everything that happens in the life of an individual is preordained. It is the result of Karma performed in the present life or in previous births. Even the worldly wise priest tells, "We poor mortals have to submit to his will." (77)

It is an age-old belief that one's fortune is determined by the position of the planets at the time of one's birth. An astrologer can predict what is going to happen in the life of an individual at various stages. Isvaran introduces a fortune teller, a Kurathi, who predicts "a sort of contamination of the body" (44) of Jagadamma.

Marital fidelity is, perhaps, the most precious and durable of the Indian values. The peculiar puritanic and holistic Indian approach to sex is one of the subsidiary themes of the story. Jagadamma is the symbol of Indian womanhood. She is satisfied with nothing short of death to one who has been contaminated, for she considers chastity as a sacred duty, "the Karma of a wife." It may appear that she committed suicide out of compulsion of her poetic sense of honour. But a deep awareness of the Hindu way of life and the duty of a Hindu wife makes her think, "Blood once fouled is fouled for ever, in the veins of wife, in the veins of mother." (58) Everything in the world has 'dharma.' The 'dharma' of a Hindu girl after marriage is faithfulness to her husband. Jagadamma could not be faithful, though not because of her fault. She is determined to drown herself not because of any sense of disappointment. She wants to purify herself by immersion in the holy waters of the Ganges. This is evident from her demeanour at the time of her immersion. She "stood behind him to be a participant in the ceremony at some of its essential points and he could scarce repress a cry of amazement at her appearance. She glowed like a Goddess. Her beauty took his breath way." (56)

Yet another important theme that Isvaran deals with in the story is the father-son relationship. Paternal love is a significant and recurring refrain as much in Isvaran's fiction as in that of his contemporaries. The patriarchal dignity in the Hindu family is one of his major themes.

From time immemorial the Hindus have been celebrating Sivaratri (the sacred night) with great devotion and piety. This occasion is associated with several religious and mythological anecdotes which given it an aura of the spiritual order of a superior level. On this occasion the devotees observe fast followed by the worship of Lord Siva all through the night. It is believed that on Sivaratri, Siva manifests himself in the form of a vast 'Linga.'

"Sivaratri" or "The Night of the Auspicious" is one of the longer stories of Isvaran in which the legend related to Lord Siva is reworked with all the suggestiveness, simplicity and grandeur of the classics in which Siva figures as one among the Hindu Trinity.

The story has three parts. The first part recounts the adventures of Lubdhaka, the hunter and his salvation through an involuntary act of worshipping a 'Sivalinga.' Lubdhaka first appears among throngs of devotees going to the shrine of Lord Siva for worship after a dip in the holy river. While the atmosphere resounds with chants of 'Siva, Siva' Lubdhaka remains totally impervious to the spirit of the people or the significance of the day. He is on his way to the woods to kill animals and birds. In the forest, strange things happen to him. Each strange experience makes him cry 'Siva! Siva!' An animal which he is about to shoot, tells him of what it was in the previous birth and the cause of its present incarnation as a doe. The doe's words bring to surface the humanity that has been lying dormant in Lubdhaka. He allows it to go. He continues his work. "The wilderness echoed to the twang of the hunter's bow string."[7] When another doe speaks to him to request him to spare it from his arrow, he obliges and lets it go. Next time it is a buck who pleads for a reprieve from death and once again he is overcome with tenderness and spares it after extracting from it a promise to return.

When Lubdhaka collects the day's kill and is about to return, the buck, and the two does with their young ones stand within his bow shot. Lubdhaka is embarrassed, as each animal in the group volunteers to be killed in order to save the others of the family. The hunter is moved to a strange pity. He seems to seek answers to the question on the secrets of life and death. "Vaguely he knew the law of life that was based on a vast reciprocal murder and that sanctified his profession." (9)

Though Lubdhaka chants the words 'Siva! Siva!' at first mockingly, they bring in him doubts which inevitably lead to knowledge. As night advances, he climbs into a bel tree to spend the night amid its branches. He has gone without food the whole day. Tormented "by hunger and benumbed with cold, he shifted his position continually on the branch, shaking down drops of dew and a few leaves and flowers and fruit, when he shifted." (10) "And Lubdhaka thought he murmured Siva! Siva! . . . the leaves and fruit fell on a Sivalinga hidden at the foot of the bel tree." (10)

In part two of the story Lord Siva explains to Uma how Lubdhaka was finally emancipated and united with 'Sivam,' the eternal. Though unconsciously, he fasted, kept vigil and offered sacrifices to Sivalinga—acts sufficient for absolution for all his past sins. Apparently the glory of Sivaratri is that your acts will be evaluated and rewarded on that night irrespective of the motivation of the acts. Renunciation precedes the unconscious offerings on the 'Sivalinga' and that paves for the hunter's salvation.

In the third part of the story Isvaran contrasts the experiences of the eighty-four-years-old grandmother observing penance with those of the younger generation. She spends the whole day fasting and chanting devotional songs and visiting shrines whereas the younger generation keep vigil at the cinema. When they return they find the old woman dead.

In contrast to the ignorant Lubdhaka, stand the other devotees who know the significance of the day. They observe fast, visit the shrines of Siva and make offerings to the idols whereas Lubdhaka quite unimpelled by any motivation cries "Siva! Siva." His acts of worship and observing fast are involuntary. The contrast between Lubdhaka and the devotees provides a deep insight into two levels of consciousness, the celestial and the mundane.

The real vitality of the story lies in the tradition of spirituality that it embodies. An attempt is made in the story to explore the secrets of the spirituality that lies in the traditional culture and their relevance in the present and its relation to the future. The author is more than an omniscient narrator in this story: he is an integral part of it.

The concept of the most marvellous of Hindu deities is presented to evoke a deepening insight into the mystery and meaning of life and its aims. There is in the story an enriching interaction between the soul of the story-teller and the eternal world.

The tale is tinged with the memory and sound and colour not only of the myths and legends related to Lord Siva but also to other episodes in Indian classics, fables, allegories and folklore that the author has imbibed from his childhood days. The story also echoes the classical episode of the transformation of the first epic poet, and the episode leading to the redemption of Ajamila, the wretched Brahmin of Kanyakubja.

The theme of the story is evidently spiritual love. Love cannot deny or bypass the reality of the physical desires, but love which never learns to go beyond the material plane knows no real fulfillment, no peace and is therefore unreal. Genuine love is deep-rooted in spirituality that transcends and dissolves itself in the infinite and eternal, and salvation is attained through death. The story also conveys the message that the clue to salvation is duty tempered with pity. Compassion is aroused by the sight of selflessness, pity and tenderness.

"The Dance of Siva" is the story of the spiritual experience of an Englishman, Peter Patterson, while returning from India, on board the ship 'Ispahan' which was moving "like a little dream town" in the Mediterranean. On board the ship Mr. Patterson cultivates the friendship of Gour Sunder De, a Bengali art dealer. They talk on Indian art as they sit in the lounge of the ship intended for First Class passengers, enjoying "full flooded Jazz tune and the 'dance of respectable ladies' and gentlemen; cocktails kindling rhythms and rhythms whirling and whispering away into the wash of the sea."[8] Patterson finds Indian art 'fantastic'; Mr. De Says, "the background of our art is our culture and without knowing the one you can't know the other. Everything in India is deeply tinged with religion." (82)

In Mr. De's cabin, Mr. Patterson sees an image of the "Tandava Nataraj," "a masterpiece of Chola sculpture." "Nataraja is Siva, one of the Hindu Trinity." He dances "to keep the equilibrium between star and star." (86) Mr. Patterson who is aware of the law of gravitation sarcastically comments, "My imagination as far as dance goes, is the jig and the hornpipe and the morris-dance of the English and the modern jazz." The dance of Siva "is a bit foggy" for him. However Mr. De feels, "the Englishman was being studiedly frivolous, even rude . . . and he wanted to strike some awe in his heart by explaining the significance of Tandava Dance." (87) Patterson listens to him.

Patterson, who has utter contempt for the dance of Siva wakes up from his sleep "to a raging cataclysm" (89) and witnesses the elemental dance of Siva in all its splendour. After the mystic experience, he visits Mr. De and apologizes for his rude behaviour.

Isvaran has a unique vision that colours his attitude towards our classical art (and literature), the products of the various stages of the evolution of Indian culture, the essence of which underlies the ritualistic, spiritual and mystic experience. The story is based on the wonderful mythology that has grown right from the Vedic period through a long and intimate tradition. In it the author embodies the whole tradition of Nataraj in its deepest and most abiding significance along with its spiritual beauty, rhythm and colour. His attitude and approach to nature, his total conception and image of Siva in His various manifestations of time and space are deeply toned and tinged by ancient Indian classics.

Koormapurana holds that Siva shows himself to each of his devotees in a shape that complies with the need of the worshipper. The story has a reference to Mankanaka, a rishi who worshipped Siva in Saptassarasvata, a place of pilgrimage in northern India. In the transport of joy on spiritual attainment, he dances. Rudra appears before him and seeks the reason behind his elated dance. Without giving a reply, he dances and dances. Rudra, seeing the rishi wrapped up in self-gratifying pleasure and conceit, resolves to deprive the devotee of his vanity, tears open his body and "dances thousand headed, thousand eyed, thousand footed, his face dreadful with fangs, flame garlanded, horrifying." After the 'tandava' the Lord resumes his former shape and reveals himself before the devotee as 'Kala' (Death) and the maker of 'Kala' (Time), and blesses Mankanaka. Patterson undergoes a similar experience at the end of which he obtains an unprecedented peace of mind. The deeper import of the dance of Nataraj is that he is the God of eternity and the God of dances. While he dances, one of his feet churns and convulses the external world and the other convulses the world of the soul in a similar manner.

Isvaran's concept of life and morality is deep-rooted in religion. The scriptures, the epics, the rituals and folk-lore which formed an integral part of his early life coupled with the observed facts of life and his personal vision created in him a deep sense of being one in a long and hallowed tradition, a sense that finds its artistic expression in these religious stories. They testify to the fact that the most dominant and enduring of the experiences which moulded the creative faculty of Isvaran is that of religion.

NOTES

1. Jawaharlal Nehru, *An Autobiography* (1936; New Delhi: Oxford UP, 1989), p. 399.
2. D. Anjaneyulu, "The Stories of Manjeri S. Isvaran," p. 13.
3. William Walsh, *Indian Literature in English* (London: Longman, 1970), pp. 7-8.
4. *Ibid.*, p. 8.
5. Isvaran, "Indian Writing," *Swatantra*, 19 September 1953, p. 30.
6. Isvaran, *Immersion* (Madras: S. Visvanathan, 1951), p. 23.
7. Isvaran, *Sivaratri* (Madras: Huxley Press, 1943), p. 4.
8. Isvaran, "The Dance of Siva," *Rickshawallah*, p. 61.

Stories: Fabulous and Mythical

Historically the fable, the parable, the folk-tale, the myth and fantasy are different genres both in style and in purpose. But Isvaran tends to combine the structural elements of these apparently varied forms to achieve his moralistic aim. He views the fabulous and the fantastic texture as an economical and effective means of revealing the interests and emotions of his characters. As in a fable, surface is relatively insignificant and exists for the sake of the meaning it carries. He also links fantasy to daydream, to egoism and escapism, in contrast with reality. The stories in which Isvaran experiments with these forms make up a considerable chunk of his literary output.

"Bewitched" is a story which combines the qualities of fable, fantasy, folk-tale, and fairy-story. It is about a mysterious doll vendor whose visit to the market-place of a little provincial town leaves an indelible impression on the minds of the people.

The doll vendor sets his basket down on the counter of the shop in the market as the shopkeeper has called him. He has got only three dolls. He makes an extravagant demand for the dolls: "a thousand mohurs each."[1] The shopkeeper cannot contain himself for laughter. He thinks that the vendor must be mad. Then the vendor summons the people round him and explains the 'mystery' about the dolls. He produces three bits of wire, and like the clever tricks of a conjurer inserts one of the wires through the left ear of the first doll and brings it out through its right. Next he pushes the second bit into the left ear of the second doll and the wire comes out through its mouth. Then he thrusts the third bit into the left ear of the third doll, but it does not emerge through any part of the doll's body. It has vanished. Now he calls upon people to explain the meaning of the phenomenon. The shopkeeper says that there is nothing to solve, for there is no riddle and that his performance is stupid. He agrees to pay the vendor three thousand mohurs if he solves the riddle. The vendor accepts the challenge and explains the mystery: the first doll stands for the principle that one must listen with one ear to everything, but must let it out through the other ear; the second one stands for listening and talking incessantly about it, and the third one means that one must listen but be quiet.

"Hardly had he finished speaking when the three dolls that stood on the counter leaped abruptly into the basket and a mist began to settle like a thick pall from end to end of the whole bazaar." (66-67) It is not known how long it lasted, but when it lifts, the vendor is nowhere to be seen. The people and the shopkeeper become "melancholy mad."

The tale has all the qualities of a fable and fairy-tale of the oral tradition combined in it. Rich imagination expressed in images drawn from our culture and a narrative directness make the story resemble a folk-tale. The fabulous quality emerges from the author's skilful construction, potent imagery, the embellished quality of his language and the overt moral element. The echo of the fairy-story is created by a fantastic atmosphere. The mystic number three is associated with the major images in the story: three dolls, three principles, three wires etc. The aura of mystery is conveyed by finely graded transitions from the normal into the strange and then beyond that into a wonderland.

Thoughtlessness, hard work, and endurance—the characteristics associated with the donkey down the ages, as depicted in numerous fables and folk-tales—have become a part of the linguistic idiom. In "Thoughtless Donkey," Isvaran reworks on an old folk-tale to illustrate his view that life "is a ceaseless quest of itself, gay, ludicrous, and tearful, cynical and ironic." (47)

The story begins in the form of a fable. The washerman's donkey born to bear "loads of linen washed and unwashed, wet and dry," (47) is also beaten severely by the washerman when he is drunk. The wrath of the washerman towards his wife and that of the wife towards the washerman are given vent to on the poor animal. The animal is not given enough to eat either. One day, when it is terribly hungry, it drinks "in one breath the whole vat of Kanji mixed with indigo." (48) When the washerman finds out what the donkey has done, he beats the animal with all his might. The animal is tortured not only when they are angry, but also when they are in a hilarious mood. As a result of drinking the blue liquid, the donkey develops a blue patch in its stomach, something that provokes the washerman and his wife "to laugh uproariously." The result is again torture.

In order to escape from the dhobi-made hell, the donkey approaches a bangle-seller. He saves the donkey from the washerman, but from the next day onwards his experience remains the same. He has to carry heavy loads and go without food. "At least the washerman's loads of linen were smooth to carry though heavy." (52) The bangle-seller carefully hides the identity of the donkey. He is afraid of losing it.

When his life with the new master becomes more and more intolerable, the poor beast thinks of going back to his old master. One day while it is coming back from a neighbouring village it meets the washerman coming from the opposite direction along the road. "The joy of the donkey knew no bounds" as also its suppressed ire against the bangle-seller "who had decoyed it to its present misery." (52) It runs forward scattering the bangles of different colours all over the road. The bangle-seller stands speechless with fury. On identifying his donkey, the washerman kicks it heartily "in a whirl of dust and oaths." (53) Then he bursts into laughter and says, "what a stu-stu-stu-peed do-o-oonkey!" (53).

The story is imbued with both facts and fancy. Fancy helps to realize the truth about life. The nature of deep musing on life and employment of fantasies lend the tale a charm of its own. Deep in Isvaran is a philosopher's mind which muses on the mystery of life and nature. He probes deeper into the mysteries of life to discover more and more of the values and aspirations of human life. The symbol of the washerman's donkey is capable of complex philosophical interpretations.

Isvaran's reflections on the forces of human destiny operating in the universe have been mixed with fine humour and a keen observation of men and matters around him. An undertone of man's protest against oppression, slavery, injustice and callousness is another hallmark of the story. But every protest takes him out of the frying pan into the burning fire. Things have been going on like this for ages.

Written in the manner of a folk-tale, "The Serpent Gem" narrates certain myths and superstitions about snakes, prevalent in rural India. At the same time the amused insight into the mind of the young lovers, Manickam and Ulundayi, and the dramatic power of the dialogue make the story a piece of high artistic order. The story was originally written by T.J. Ranganathan in Tamil which later Isvaran translated into English. John Hampson observes, "It is a tragedy told with poetic elegance and imagination."[2]

Ulundayi, who believes that "the snake was a garland round the neck of Lord Siva, the snake was the couch of Lord Vishnu,"[3] would manage to make the snake that "dwells beneath the jasmine bush vomit the gem out of its mouth." (138-39) But fate wills otherwise; Manickam is bitten by the same snake and he dies. She is not able to bear the sorrow. She laments, "Sinner that I am, I asked for the serpent gem, and asking for it lost the most precious of all gems!" (140)

The last story "The Serpent Expiates" forms the sequel wherein Isvaran provides a happy ending for Ulundayi. Manickam who is supposed to be dead comes to life. He marries Ulundayi, "who firmly believes that the serpent of its own free will had taken back its poison and resurrected the dead." (155)

"A Bold Stroke," a story told by the narrator's aunt Lakshmi to a band of children belonging to different families, assembled in a house to attend a marriage, begins in the manner of an old folk-tale. It is about the miserable experiences and sorrow of a beautiful young wife, caused by her husband who "didn't care for her, ignored her very presence in the house."[4] Despite her patience and the discharge of domestic duties to please him he turns his back on her. He keeps himself away from the house most of the time. Advised by a well-meaning old lady of the neighbourhood who tries to rescue her, the young wife follows her husband and finally succeeds in winning him over. The narrator, who listens to the aunt eagerly at a distance, realizes that the story is meant for a man, who has abandoned his wife just as the man in the story has done, some fifteen years ago. The story over, he hangs down his head in shame and goes out.

"Illumination" is more like a fable, but nonetheless wholesome and natural in its effect on the readers. It appeals to the sense of fun and like a traditional fable the significance of the story is embodied in actions dramatized in dialogue and represented by images of meaningful objects. The story deals with the revenge of a bull calf, Nandi, about nine months old, and the cowherd Kannan "a rogue and a heartless fellow" who "has killed many calves." (82) Nandi observes, "Every moment he looks at me I see murder in his eyes." (84) One day Nandi knocks him down and makes him roll "across gravel and stones and knots of harsh grass bruising his bare breast, arms, face, fingers, legs, his cloth torn and falling off his waist and wet with stains of blood and dirt." (85) He is hospitalized by the master who is very kind to him during his stay in the hospital. Then one day, "A sudden illumination had come upon his mind. He hadn't done his duty by the cows. He has starved the calves, denied them their mother's milk." (87)

When he comes back from the hospital he is a changed man. He calls the cows affectionately by their pet names. The animals low gently in answer and look up as though they understand. Nandi too begins to love him. One day "before he went for the udder of his mother he licked his cheek slowly, tenderly, his tongue, flicking close under his right eye. The piece of plaster fell off and the skin shone healthy without a scar. Kannan wished no more to die, darling Nandi had given him the sanction for a new life." (88) The tale is put in the rural background with a tender domestic touch.

The creative vision of Isvaran, rooted in the cultural and traditional values of the society to which he belongs, considers superstition an integral part of the society. Introducing the story "Sivaratri," Isvaran writes: "What the world is in need of today is a dynamic superstition which will destroy the lies of equivocations of the intellect and re-discover the human heart. Our myths are dynamic superstitions." In individual and social life Isvaran believes that tradition and culture have infinite connotations. The superstitions, especially those related to folklore and religion form an integral part of our culture, and is manifest variously in the stories of Isvaran.

"The Miracle of the Door" is a story based on superstition, a rework of an old story, familiar to Isvaran as told by his old grandmother. Like a fable the story "contains moral as bright as mirrors."[5] The distancing of the story from the contemporaneity by means of the technique of folk-tale explains away what appears irrational. It is the story of a Brahmin housewife who, because of the pressure of circumstances, underpays the domestic servants and even cheats one who is blind. She dies at the age of forty. When the dead body is taken for funeral, it is dropped on the bare floor at the threshold of the house by those who carry it. They see something which hinders them on the way. A hush of supernatural fear descends on those present. An old widow in the crowd announces, "Lakshmi has not paid a debt and when she pays it, out she will go. In life she did not pay, in death she must." (10) The widow's words are carried out and "something very dark and massive as a wall that blocked the doorway vanished." (12) Its brevity, compression and the focus on a moral, make the story resemble a fable.

"The Cradle" is based on the operation of superstition among the common people. The story centres round an empty cradle in the house of a lower middle-class woman Kalyani, who looks much older than what she really is on account of the sorrow caused by the death of her three children. She later realizes that a child had died in the cradle before she bought it. She thinks that the spirit of the child has "caused the death of more children, her darling ones, one after another"[6] as they were put in the cradle.

One of Isvaran's most characteristic traits is that of finding the elements of superstition in the everyday commonplace life that is continually going on around him. His creative genius is characterized by a large proportion of feminine elements, depth and tenderness of feeling, purity of mind and certain grace and vivacity in narrating incidents and delineating characters. The strength of beauty of a mother's love permeate this exquisite piece.

Although Isvaran is proud of India's past, he seems a little unhappy with certain religious superstitions which bring about unnecessary tension and mental agony at least to certain sections. Such superstitions are rooted in myths and legends.

The theme of the story, "At His Nativity," is the tension on the part of certain orthodox people caused by the popular belief among the Hindus that a male child born on the auspicious hour when Srikrishna was born under the star Rohini, would be inauspicious to his uncle. The idea of the story is built round such a situation of childbirth, into which Isvaran weaves tradition and beliefs. The woman delivers the baby exactly at "the hour when Srikrishna was born."[7] The genuine tension on the part of the grandmother and the mother of the woman who delivers is presented with the insight of a psycho-analyst.

Another aspect of superstition is dealt with in the story "Sea Shells" in which figures the sad and young widow Syamala whose husband lost his life while taking a dip in the sea "on a day when there was an eclipse of the moon."[8] He had taken the advice of his priest who maintained that "the serpent had hitched its tail" (45) to his star. The priest had advised him to bathe in the sea "with the charm of the palmirah leaf tied over his brow," (45) as it would surely save him from some imminent star-imposed tragedy.

Based on and controlled by an overt violation of what is generally accepted as possible or probable, a literary fantasy explains meanings or realities behind what is apparent. It pulls the reader from the everyday world of reality to the realm of a marvellous world where he will be exposed to strange experiences which would in turn help him in the realization of his own world. "Visit of an Immortal" is a literary fantasy written in the interest of box office, on the noble concepts and the grandeur of classical literature and culture.

Svarnakumari, "the darling of the masses, the blazing new star,"[9] plays the titular role in "Sakuntala," the smashing hit of the pingala for the season. (54) Tonight she must give her best in bringing out to the full all the simplicity, all the artless charm of the forest maiden Sakuntala. She has done well in the rehearsals. The director is satisfied. The make-up artist has done his best to make her appear in her first bloom that night, though she is much past it. When she is alone in the room in the full make-up of Sakuntala she opens the note-book containing the dialogue. Before she opens the book, she sees a hallucination or a dream or illusion, the Sakuntala of Kalidasa.

The apparition bursts out on Svarnakumari for desecrating her name, and tarnishing her "immortal glory." She tells, "As Sakuntala you are dragging me to the dirt, me, poet Kalidasa's Sakuntala." (58) Svarnakumari makes a confession of her ignorance of Kalidasa and Sakuntala. She tells that the story in which she is featured as Sakuntala is written by one Subbanna, the dialogue is by Pappanna, and the songs are by their popular composer Soma Sarma. She confesses, "In plain life

I am Kannamma, daughter of Alamelu." (58) Svarnakumari thinks that these songs "are really, hits" (60) and sings a piece for Sakuntala, who finds it a horrible experience. ". . . the fervour and ache in the tone of her celestial visitor proved so overwhelming that she was all attention, with cheek on palm and the dawn of a new understanding in her eyes." (60) She takes a hurried glance in the mirror. She sees half her chin smudged red from down the corner of her mouth. The lip-salve has flowed out. With a quick mortification she realizes how absent-mindedly she has poured herself out a cup of coffee. This startles Sakuntala. Finally the actress confesses that she is all make-up. Sakuntala replies, "I never painted myself, I never decked myself in tawdry stuff. I am Kalidasa's Sakuntala. O! if you must play my part on the earth, be Kalidasa's Sakuntala. Don't desecrate my name. Don't insult the poet." (60) Then the celestial shape disappears.

The story embodies Isvaran's righteous indignation at vulgarizing the beauty, nobility and simplicity of the Sakuntala of Kalidasa's classic world. His passionate admiration for Kalidasa and deep insight into his genius are brought forth in his contrast of the two worlds, the world depicted by Kalidasa, and its poor and degrading imitation by the cine-artists. In order to dramatize the contrast of the two worlds, he resorts to fantasy, and his choice is artistically effective.

When the story opens, we see the protagonist in a world of reality, in an ordinary state of mind, which under psychic influence soon takes on an 'eerie' character that enables her to see the marvellous world of Sakuntala, in a fantasy. Here fantasy aims at bringing forth the absolute meaning that lies in the classical work of art in contrast to its vulgarized version. This aim of Isvaran's use of fantasy is necessarily the depiction of reality which cannot be done by using the conventional methods.

Yet another story which is a fine example of Isvaran's art of blending fantasy with fun is "Angry Dust." It is the story of Adam Khan, "fifty eight, six foot four, dressed in immaculate white and white ribbon"[10] now employed as a duffedar to a British officer. Adam Khan had a very brilliant and glorious career in the army. As he sits on his stool outside the door of the officer, someone "whispered in his ear that the dress that he wore was the dress that the great Moghuls had worn with pride and magnificence for nearly two centuries." (66) The very mention of Moghul glory evokes a fantasy in which,

> [he] saw the pomp and splendour of the royal court; the gorgeous mehals overflowing with gems and gold that the vassals laid as tribute at the feet of their sovereign; the Wazirs and Amirs arrayed in their best . . . his face turned to Mecca, calling the faithful

> to prayer; it made his breath catch in a species of transport and tears of happiness filled his eyes. (66-67)

He is awakened from the reverie when the bell twitters inside the room. The illusion is suddenly broken reducing the 'Great Moghul' to the level of an old, bent, servile office peon.

In this group of stories, fantasy and reality are so inextricably combined that the aura of mystery conveyed is finely graded transitions from the normal into the strange and then beyond that into the marvellous. However, in his role as a fabulist Isvaran does not discard his garb of a moralist. Unconcealed disgust at protest against the social squalor and wretchedness that he saw around him find imaginative treatment in most of his stories. In these stories, as in a fable, surface is relatively insignificant and exists for the sake of the meaning it carries—the author's moral purposefulness and the consequential didactic tone.

NOTES

1. *Rickshawallah*, p. 64.
2. Introduction, *No Ankletbells for Her*, p. xv.
3. *No Ankletbells for Her*, p. 129.
4. *Painted Tigers*, p. 93.
5. *Angry Dust*, p. 1.
6. *Naked Shingles*, p. 123.
7. *No Ankletbells for Her*, p. 21.
8. *Naked Shingles*, p. 44.
9. *Rickshawallah*, p. 54.
10. *Angry Dust*, p. 62.

Stories as Lyrics

A short story that is finely wrought has the richness and conciseness of an excellent lyric, for it is "a form that often attracts the talents of poets whose gifts make them generally masters of this form of writing. Walter de la Mare, Stephen Spender, Dylan Thomas, Robert Graves and William Plommer for example have each given brilliant demonstrations of their skill in the art."[1] It has been generally accepted that "to the poetic mind everything is poetic."[2] To Edgar Allan Poe, whose achievement as a short story writer and poet remains undisputed, "the ideal creative opportunity is offered by lyric poem and the short tale."[3] Valerie Shaw in her stimulating introduction to *The Short Story* observes that the "closest literary ancestor (of the subjective short stories) is the lyric form perfected by Browning who managed to fuse character, action and setting within individual poetic monologues making one speaker's words carry the entire burden of meaning and leaving the reader or supposed listener to make his own interpretation." (105) A lyrical short story in which the writer employs fictional devices to find an aesthetic expression for his experiences has to be considered genuine poetry. "The modern short story writer," says Walter Allen, "is a lyric poet in prose and indeed the effect on the reader of many modern short stories, those of Chekhov conspicuously, is nearer to that of lyric poetry than to that of the novel or of older stories."[4] Isvaran himself has said, "English literature has some of its best prose written by poets."[5] Nancy Hale defines short story as "a lyric cry in the face of human destiny."[6]

Lyric as we know has its genesis in a spontaneously melodic expression, which in course of time adapted itself to ritualistic need, and became formalized music in folk-lore, epic and the dramatic. A lyric in the modern sense of the form assumes very complex and manifold combinations—of formal music, of words with all their meanings and associations, of mental and external pictures, of qualities of thought and feeling, emotion and sensation, of deep awareness of the past, present and future. These qualities which seem to be unconnected attributes find a conglomeration in the lyric. Unifying and interpreting them in accordance with the varied themes and moods of the story lie in the creative faculty of the artist. Brevity, metrical coherence, subjectivity, passion, sensuality and particularity of image, which characterize the lyric genre, form the features of a good short story. On this feature of the short story Eileen Baldeshwiler observes: "In present day literary theory, the term 'lyric' refers of course not so much to structure as to subject and tone, and it is mainly to these aspects of the brief narrative that the adjective is meant to call attention in the phrase 'lyrical' story."[7] A lyrical story maintains the essentials of story telling, such as characters, theme, plot, narrative etc. and the medium remains prose.

A critical analysis of Isvaran's stories and poems reveals that his capabilities lie deeply rooted in the tradition of the Brahminical culture of south India. The rich spiritual and ritualistic atmosphere that was peculiar to that culture gave Isvaran as a boy, opportunities to be exposed to the chanting of verse from the Upanishads, hymns from the Vedas, recitation and interpretation of the puranas and epics. The other early influences which shaped the poetic sensibilities were the Malayalam and Tamil folk songs and folk-lore. All these left deep and abiding impression on the sensibilities of young Isvaran. On account of the socio-economic and political scenario of the country, Isvaran happened to choose English as the medium of his creative expression leaving behind his mother tongue Tamil and his foster language Malayalam. Isvaran's major attitudes and approaches to life, nature, society and individual characters take clear and definite shape in his stories rather than in his poems, though poetry happened to be his first love.

His personal reactions and responses at the depth of his being are all-pervasive and find splendid expression in his stories. As a story-teller, he conveys high excitements and profound effects comparable only to those created in lyric poetry. Delicate and incorruptible emotions, powerful and independent mind, both of them with the sensibility of the poet are truly reflected in the creative mirror of Isvaran's imagination. Isvaran's entire system as a story-teller is based on the lyrical element. That is perhaps what prompted Irene Coates to observe, "It is hard to speak of Mr. Isvaran's poems without calling to mind his stories, since similar moods and subjects are found in each."[8] The stories show Isvaran's most compulsive fictional impulses at work leading towards a ballad-like impersonality and artistic autonomy. What has been said of Chekhov, "architectonics of his stories is akin to that of a musical composition,"[9] is true of the well-built stories of Isvaran.

Despite the medium of modern short story to which the literature, art, religion, ethics, metaphysics and aesthetics of the Orient are alien, in Isvaran's creative faculty they become an integral part. This is perhaps the reason of his identifying the Hindu way of life as the theme of his major stories. And it is not surprising that his prototypical patterns are of Hindu religion.

Through this chosen medium he was able to explore the possibilities of prose as a medium experimenting with rhythm, cadence and isocolon in a style which the modern Western poets and the Indian classics mark significantly. Commenting on the short stories of William Samson, Isvaran observes, "his present writing while it cannot be acknowledged as prose poetry or poetic prose must be called (meaning no offence) as a cross between prose and verse . . . the effect it produces is that of a strange kind of poetry fascinating for its rhythm."[10] This is true of Isvaran's stories too. But in the case of Isvaran, his language is capable of creating a high degree of nature which is the soul of all true poetry. He writes his stories in a prose constantly verging on poetry as he evokes the past times. Like real poetry, Isvaran's short story invites many views from different perspectives. No one measurement can ever take all the diverse dimensions of the masterpieces.

Like a lyric poem, a typical short story of Isvaran requires the reader's utmost attention, a focussing of the mind on each detail in order to realize the final fullness of effect. It depends on concreteness, on sensual impressions that deliver their meaning without waste. It stays within the world it creates.

If folk-lore and the Sanskrit classics and the early domestic atmosphere of meditation and rituals helped in the blossoming of his imaginative vision, his acquaintance with the modern Indian as well as the Western literature gave it new dimensions. As a journalist, Isvaran had opportunity to review the works of his contemporaries in the West. He reviewed the works of Robert Graves, E.M. Forster, Wallace Stevens, George Orwell, L.A.G. Strong, Irene Coates, Edith Sitwell, Galsworthy, D.H. Lawrence, Laurie Lee and Stephen Spender. There seems to be no better way of making oneself acquainted with the art of a writer than reviewing his works. Isvaran did this job quite earnestly after having practised the art of short story, for over a decade.

The American, Russian, French and English models of short stories supplied Isvaran with techniques and patterns for the delineation of Indian life. K.S. Venkataramani observes: "Mr. Isvaran is essentially a poet, but the temper and urges of the renascent India make him a story-teller. When a poet becomes a story-teller, the chances are that poetic gifts lie in his story like nuggets of gold in river sand untouched by the craftsmanship of the story-teller. Generally the gifts of the poet and the story-teller lie apart. At best it is only a sweet embrace. But in Mr. Isvaran's art there is a fusion of the gifts and the result is integral."[11] K. Chandrasekharan, a contemporary of Isvaran and a well-known critic, observes: "Sri Isvaran all along concentrated mainly on two media of self-expression, poems and short stories in English though the dividing line between the two happens in his case to become more imaginary than real. For the substance of his thought always remains poetical."[12] A delicate taste and quick perception which create the fine touches of feeling and fancy, a brilliant and bold imagination and beautiful simplicity and elegance of style place him among the very first of Indian short story writers in English.

The term lyrical implies to a single thought, feeling or situation.[13] It appeals more to the heart than to the intellect. James E. Miller and Bernice Slot rightly point out: "the short story offers a very special challenge, comparable, say, to a sonnet as compared to a long narrative poem. Indeed short story writers from Poe to Faulkner have believed that the finest stories are closer in technique to poetry than to novel. There are density of meaning, richness of texture, compactness of form in both lyric poetry and short story."[14] Poe has even gone to the extent of saying, "the tale has a point of superiority even over the poem."[15]

The term lyric technically refers to a method as well as an effect. The method entails sequential action and gradual increase in intensity. These two lyric methods are manipulated by the following lyric devices.

1. Arrangement of events to emphasize their effect on the reader, i.e. a movement in outer action, counterpointed by a movement in inner life.
2. A dialogue that is ritualistic or non-ritualistic, capable of creating the desired atmosphere and mood.
3. The revelation, which is the point of the story, is achieved by an effective reader participation.
4. The effective use of symbols and images to embody and dramatize themes.
5. Proper use of poetic devices such as suggestiveness to achieve the desired effects.

While commenting on certain aspects of lyric, Barbara Hardy points out: "the advantage of lyric in itself is its concentrated and patterned expression of feeling. This advantage is negatively definable: the lyric does not provide an explanation or judgment or narrative; what it does provide is feeling alone, without histories or characters."[16] Isvaran as a short story writer makes the best use of this advantage. In his case there is a gradual development from lyric poetry to short fiction. The triumph of Isvaran's short fiction appears to be his concept of the language of the lyric and short story. To quote R.F. Dietrich and Ruger M. Sundell: "Unlike the scientific language of observation and report, the language of fictional literature is a total language. It employs such devices as rhythm, metaphor, image, symbol, plot, character, setting, tone and point of view to convey feelings and express ideas that will appeal to the whole man—to his senses, emotions, imagination and intellect."[17]

What is significant in Isvaran's stories is not situations, nor even characters—though characters and temperaments are also brought out in the clearest of lines and contours—but his mood and feeling and atmosphere. Like the sweet embrace of the melody of a song, these evanescent moods, feelings and atmosphere and revelations linger in the reader long after the story is read. It is the atmosphere, the mood, and the tone that impart a meaning to the total theme of his work. If in the story "Bewitched" it is an atmosphere of mystery, in "Revelation" it is one of romantic longings.

The structure of most of the early stories resembles a symbolist poem in which the narrative framework remains nominal, the main focus being on a series of images, introduced through the technique of an omniscient third-person narrator's reverie and his personal comments. The images cohere and combine to evoke the particular mood, subjective emotion and the external scene being fused with varying degrees of skill.

The stories of Isvaran's first collection, *Naked Shingles*, are primarily concerned with mood or atmosphere and events happens outside the boundaries of the story itself. Mood as a fictional device used by Isvaran is the attitude of a character to an object, to a situation, or to a person figuring in that particular work. The story, "Jowramma," for example, movingly delineates the deepest moods and moments in the life of a simple rural belle. In these early stories, Isvaran exploits background and landscape to convey this mood. The title story, for example, begins with a description of the sea and the sky: "Far, far, away, where the sea and sky mated under a luminous haze, roses were beginning to bloom. The sea lay as smooth as glass, the wind was still. At this early hour of dawn the Triplicane Beach presented a scene of quiet loveliness."[18] In Isvaran's hands, this description has ceased to be an ordinary description of nature. It has absorbed the colour, fragrance and the hushed tranquillity of an autumn day. "Merry Go Round," the story with which the volume opens, is the portrayal of a poignant human situation in colourful phrasing and imagery. "The Dance of Siva," the story of a strange experience of an Englishman on board a ship in the Mediterranean, contains a description of nature quite in keeping with the theme of the story: "Under a waxing moon the sombre waters began to pale, the shadows shook over their flowering buds of light, and slowly the Mediterranean opened out in full silver splendour, unfurling fabric after fabric of memories of its historic past. And the Ispahan moved like a little dream town, through waters that never seemed to end, through memories turning turbulent under a waxing moon."[19]

Isvaran presents his characters always in their highest and deepest moods of feeling. The most fascinating of Isvaran's tales seldom tells a tale but depicts a scene or presents a situation either to illuminate a mood or perpetuate a moment. Such stories scarcely carry any plot in the conventional sense and hardly any action worth the name. Nothing happens in them, so there is no question of wanting to know what happens next. They lack the element of suspense. As a matter of fact, what goes on inside his characters—their inner life—is highlighted, rather than what happens on the surface. The strength of Isvaran as a storyteller lies precisely in this capacity. "Mythili" is the story of a sensitive young husband involved in a humiliating situation and his immediate reaction to the situation and final realization of his folly. The change in the husband's mood from blind fury to repentance and love is presented with a few touches of delicate irony which enrich the drama of varied emotions. Similarly "Last Pawn" presents an entirely predictable situation. A desperate proletarian woman pawns her ear-rings in vain to save her only child. "Sea Shells" is a tragic and dream-filled story that illustrates Isvaran's poetry of fear. "The War Memorial" is a story of paternal attitudes. Isvaran's was genuinely the quick sensitive mind of a poet, and the stories take on their quality from the characteristic lyrical impulse of that mind.

The spiritual insight and metaphysical content in accordance with the varied themes and moods make Isvaran's stories stand out from those of his contemporaries. In "Immersion," which is widely considered to be Isvaran's magnum opus, this metaphysical content and the mood of reverie pervading the entire story are evoked first by a folk song of Malabar, sung by the cartman who later in the story turns out to be the villain of the piece. Towards the end of the folk song, the author reflects solioquously: "When will the plant flower? . . . floated the burden of the song wistfully. If only the mood behind such songs remained wistful for ever, longing fondly for the ideal! But alas, how thin is the division between the dream for the ideal feminine and the building desire for the female flesh!"[20] The narrator who is at times the commentator and a silent and passive participant in the scheme of things knows well what is in store for the characters. The song sets him on a psychological probe into the longings and romantic dreams and aspirations of the youth and provides hints on the possible and the probable. "The magic and miracle of youth! Throwing the rainbow woof of yearnings over the warp of romance! To it a moment waiting for love is an eternity and with love on its hands eternity a moment." (6) The mood peculiar to this part of the story is created by a description of the scene:

"It was a night of peculiar charm, potential for peculiar happenings, when nature is a little doubtful of her moods, doubtful which way to plunge into playfulness and gaiety or don the sable of tragedy." (2)

What makes him wonder at the beauty and mystery of the eternal universal life is perhaps the melody of the song. The magic of the ancient in sound and colour in all the wonder and beauty of nature and seasons are brought forth in the story, by reference to the local lore of the "Umbrella Stone." The very sight of the stone prompts Akhileswaran plunge into a reverie. He reflects: "Folk-lore is so redolent of rustic piety and innocence that it is timid before reason, and thrives only on man's complicity, this short digression but intensified his anxiety relating to more important matters." (9) What he seeks to explore beneath the outward and trivial happenings is this immortal glory and nobility of human soul. In the story the author shows an introspective spirit, the high sensibility given to the enjoyment of the mystery of life.

The duration of the stories, offers the reader, in the characteristic manner of a lyric, a segment excised from the flow of time, a moment and a mood held still, yet filled with fleeting memories or half-formed regrets. In this respect Isvaran agrees with the view of Sherwood Anderson, "the short story is the result of a sudden passion."[21]

Isvaran is not concerned with what is conventionally accepted as important moments in a work of fiction. So he generally avoids such blood-curdling things as murder, suicide and incidents which exercise a terrible impact on his characters, though the stories "Painted Tigers" and "Overwrought" prove that he is capable of depicting such things. On the other hand, he believes that the essence of life could be held in moments of transient emotion.

Isvaran considers that "the writer is honoured because he represents a kind of 'mystery' of the mind. He is a wonder worker who carries around in his head the portals to the worlds. He can make a world in which the reader may live, if he wants to, for two or three hours and hold the memory of the experience for as long as he likes."[22] The sense of mystery that he presents often associates itself with the idea of an absolute external reality, something that art cannot touch, but only reveal. The centrality of the stories of Isvaran, especially those dealing with the Hindu way of life, is this mystery.

"Every good story has a mystery," says Eudora Welty, "not the puzzle kind, but the mystery of allurement. As we understand the story better, it is likely that the mystery does not necessarily increase; rather it simply grows more beautiful."[23] The beauty of Isvaran's stories emanates from a certain quality of their atmosphere which lifts the commonplace and ordinary characters to a world of strange, sensuous sphere. This endows them with a subtle and powerful emotional balance, a soft and plaintive tenderness and a glow of joy and pain. In "No Ankletbells for Her," Annakkili "the child of the gutters," is fascinated by "catching her reflection in the croup of the car"[24] and begins to dance. For a moment she forgets all about the gruesome monotony, the filth and squalor, poverty and the cruelty of her mother and is transported to a world of beauty and rhythm:

> Maybe she remembered vaguely when she smiled, the painted eunuchs she had been dancing before shopfronts during the pongal festival. No ballerina that pirouetted on a stage that changed under changing lights and shadows, with an auditorium bewitched before her starry eyes and the symphony of the orchestra falling divinely on her ears, no devadasi that did her Natya in front of the decorated idol of god or goddess could have been so ecstatic as was this child of the gutters. She danced. The open road was her audience, the din of traffic her background music. She danced, her gaiety unabated, for gaze fixed on the rear of the car. (3)

Similarly "Jowramma" resembles a pastoral poem. It illustrates how deep is Isvaran's insight into the simple unostentatious life of the rustic people in their simple and sincere love and their incapacity to hate. Mali, the young farmer, is in love with the soil as much as he loves his wife, Jowramma. A mysterious relation exists between the simple village folk and nature. Jowramma's feminine whims and fancies, and womanly frailty do not allow her to be so much aware of it as Mali. His deep interest in nature is tinged with intimately personal emotions.

Jowramma, who reaches the railway station to leave for Madras with the Under Secretary's family, experiences 'a tremor' in her heart, "a giddiness in her head" and a "hectic gleam in her eyes." What is more,

> She seemed to see her husband toiling lonely in the farm in the cold wind and dense fog and pelting rain, cooking his food, tending the cows, lonely, desolate. And she saw him outlined against the immense toga of mist, moving from patch to patch, moving as it were along the margin of the world, the earth lying like a smoking mummy under a melancholy sky with trees rising naked and boughless and like spectres in pale grey waste, and she saw his sad face looming and unnatural, his eyes chiding her disobedience and desertion. She stifled a sob in her throat whilst the tears distilled deep in her heart, her boy tight to her bosom and picking up the bundle made for the exit.[25]

The stories of Isvaran which depict the life of the countryfolk contain passages similar to the one cited above, showing his deep attachment to the great spaces of earth and sky, the boundless horizon, the expanse of moonlight, assuming varied colours and forms in tune with the moods of his characters.

An entranced and blissful contemplation of nature and a dream-like atmosphere that mark an intense and inseparable bond connecting man with nature characterize the rustic stories of Isvaran, thereby contributing to their lyrical excellence. As for the description of nature he seems to agree with the view of Chekhov, "descriptions of nature should be very brief and have an incidental character."[26]

A sense of overpowering destiny is generated by the land in Thomas Hardy's novels. In each of them, nature plays the role of a significant character. Similarly, in those of Isvaran's stories that deal with the relation of man and nature, nature plays a significant role. In "Immersion," it is the cart, a passive observer of the evil contrivances of the cartman that becomes instrumental in taking revenge. On the other hand, in "Jowramma" it is nature which directs the innocent rustic girl to the right path of reunion with her husband without any ill-feeling. In stories like "Jowramma," "Naked Shingles," "Sivaratri" and "Immersion," the vision of man and nature comes together, adding much more to their majesty and significance. In them the word-pictures have often a particularity which gives them a charming completeness and individuality, revealing minute traits which the reader immediately and pleasantly recognizes.

In Isvaran's stories, statements are not explicit, but invariably implicit. This superb suggestiveness contributes significantly to their lyrical effect. In "The Role of the Story-teller in the Modern World," Isvaran observes, "there is no better illustration of literary capacity in suggestion and imaginative incandescence than can be found in a good short story."[27] Round the word-pictures of Isvaran, in his stories, cluster, suggestions and evocations, and every line, every word, every gesture and even the structure itself work in suggestiveness. Eminent practitioners of the art of short fiction have expressed more or less similar views. For example, R.B. West and R.W. Stallman write: "All fiction exists somewhere between the poles of realism which stresses an extreme fidelity to nature and symbolism which subordinates 'reality' and emphasizes a theme or meaning which is suggested by events or characters."[28] Conrad's view is not much different either. He observes: "All art, therefore, appeals primarily to the senses, and the artistic aim when expressing itself in written words must also make its appeal through the senses, if its high desire is to reach the secret spring of responsive emotions. It must strenuously aspire to the plasticity of sculpture, to the colour of painting, and to the magic suggestiveness of music—which is the art of arts."[29] Sean O'Faolain says: "Telling by means of suggestion or implication is one of the most important of all modern short story's shorthand convention."[30]

Quite often in Isvaran's stories the aura of suggestion radiates from a definite meaning relating to the world he depicts and its full significance is not seen until the essential attitude of the story is grasped. This tends to intense concentration, simplicity and reticence of expression. In "Angry Dust" the author takes recourse to fantasy and dream to suggest the atmosphere of Moghul splendour. Literary fantasy is made use of by Isvaran for the manifestation of unconscious desires and fears. His use of fantasy in this story is different from the utopian fantasies of the fairy tale or the religious myth or the romance. On the other hand, it represents a refracted world, transformed through the mind of the perceiver and his or her unconscious projections into the world.

As a fantasy, the "Visit of an Immortal" turns out to be a vehicle by which the author dramatizes ideas of high seriousness. It is a potent tool in the hands of Isvaran who wishes to satirize the film world. At the same time, it clarifies the inner workings of the heroine's soul.

The awful world that enshrines the concept of Siva in "The Dance of Siva" sets another example of Isvaran's superb handling of suggestion and the fantasy of the religious myth. It transcends the bounds of known reality and conjures up a strange and marvellous world, devoted to presenting human life in terms of social and societal realities. One can hardly come across an Indian English short story which is as suggestive as "Immersion," for the whole story moves on a series of subtle suggestions. What actually happens between the cartman and Jagada, while Akhileswaran is away in search of the pot of ashes, has nowhere been stated, but only suggested, despite its being the cause of the tragedy. The intensity of the excruciating agony of Jagada is reflected in her anguished face and stiffened movements.

A definitive melancholy-yearning forms the undertone of all stories of Isvaran. This arises from a rich intuition and the subtlety of observation going to the heart of the characters and situations he depicts. His genius had been shaped by Indian culture, though in course of his development as a writer he was fostered by the Western thought as well. Isvaran writes, "When there is pure music there is melancholy—like a dream broken abruptly, but for ever remembered, and music is the deepest of the arts and deep beneath the arts."[31]

A sensitive soul making a keen perception of the world of Isvaran's stories comes across a mood of unmixed beauty touched with a sense of pain and loss. All this is enveloped in the collective consciousness of a people of fabulous cultural heritage manifest in their myths, legends, folk songs and folk-tales. Isvaran often turns to them to give a specific shape and significance to the vision of his men and world. The melancholic quality of his vision and his ironic understanding of life have been manifest in all his stories irrespective of their theme and treatment.

This brings us closer to the personality of the author and his main preoccupations. The cause of the prevalent pensiveness of these stories is always evocative and self-explanatory. Most of the stories of Isvaran do not take the reader forward into a unique eventuality, but refer him back to the customs, conventions, folklore, myth or legend or some flaw or impulsive act on the part of the protagonist. In "Immersion," the prevailing melancholy mood of the protagonist is caused by his inability to be present at home in the last hours of his father and later for his funeral. This happens not because of his fault. However, he becomes more enthusiastic in carrying out 'the Immersion ceremony' unblemished. In "Crutches" it is the characteristic jealousy of a young woman that leaves another woman of her age in lifelong suffering. Her sense of guilt makes her entire life cloudy. The protagonist of the story, "The Man behind the Chair," leaves home and does not write to his parents for two years, for he is unaware of the sorrow and anxiety of his parents. He, on the other hand, wants to make a pleasant surprise by appearing before them with the riches he has earned. The parents die of grief leaving the protagonist to suffer the pangs of a sense of guilt that haunts him throughout his life. What pains him more than the loss of his wife and children and his fortunes in the 'Quetta earthquake' seems to be this. The undertone of melancholy transcends into hazy sentimentalism in stories like "Last Pawn" where the cause of suffering and the sorrow of the poor working class woman is not only the divine providence but the cruelty of man towards man.

Stories like "Merry Go Round," "The Last Pawn," "The Motorman" and "Immersion" are characterized by melancholy and melodrama on account of the archetypal situation that they set forth: the miserable condition of women through generations.

Intensity, an outstanding characteristic of his stories, is in fact a reflection of his hypersensitive nature and his highly emotional temperament. Whatever be the state of mind that he presents, there is inevitably an exuberance of emotion in its delineation. It makes his language vivid and renders his images strikingly poetic.

Yet another poetic device that Isvaran employs successfully in his short stories is allegory. According to West and Stallman, "a story becomes allegorical only when the symbols are used constantly to signify a second series of events in all of its important details. If only isolated symbols are used to suggest the events symbolized the story is not allegorical, but it is symbolic." It is an "unambiguous hewing, a clearly consistent path in which all details, both on the factual and on the symbolic level agree."[32] In "Immersion" the question is whether he intended it to be an allegory with all the events and objects fitted perfectly into the details which we know of the story in the *Ramayana*, which tells the contamination of Sita or whether he meant to suggest through a body of images and symbols, the general philosophical beliefs which are understood to be illustrated through the story of Rama and Sita for the most important episodes in the story have to be taken not at the factual level alone, but at another—a symbolic as well as allegorical—level. There are clear hints of this at the very beginning of the story. Given this hint the problem of reading the story becomes much more complex. Anyway the reader has to think of the story in terms of the *Ramayana*. This is a concept which the author knew and utilized from his own background of religion and classical literature, a concept which saw beauty of life as purity and innocence which saw death as the only way of purification from contamination. A close examination of the details in "Immersion" reveals that Isvaran has depicted the idea by juxtaposing the world of his art with that of the ancient Indian classics. Judging from these standards, the story has to be taken as a kind of religious allegory. In stories like "Angry Dust," "Visit of an Immortal" and "The Dance of Siva," his main preoccupation is with the world of dream and fantasy.

"Sivaratri," a bold experiment of Isvaran in the genre he has chosen as his literary medium, glorifies human feelings of love and compassion. The narration of the tale bears the essential characteristic of a fable—brevity, compression of facts, simplicity of language, presentation of animal characters in the extension of jungle life bearing the human situation. Each animal and human being in the story, in the characteristic manner of fable, has stock allegorical attributes.

As a writer of lyrical stories, Isvaran belongs to the tradition of Turgenev, Chekhov, A.E. Coppard and Katherine Mansfield. Among the Indian short story writers in English, he is essentially an innovator, who, while maintaining all that is best in the long tradition of Indian tales, goes beyond them to enrich the genre with lyrical elements. The integrity of his poetic eye and imagination is such that it penetrates into the core of persons, places and things. He rejects all embellishments and presents the essentials with a singular charm, simplicity and power. As a short story writer, Isvaran is a class by himself.

NOTES

1. John Hampson, Introduction, *No Ankletbells for Her*, p. 9.
2. Henry Wordsworth Longfellow, *Hawthorne and the Critical Heritage* (London: Routledge and Kegan Paul, 1970), p. 56.
3. Randall Stewart and Dorothy Bethurun, *Classic American Fiction* (Chicago: Scott Foresman, 1954), p. 3.
4. *The Short Story in English* (Oxford: Clarendon Press, 1981), p. 8.
5. Rev. of "Rose for Winter: Travels in Andalusia" by Laurie Lee, *Swatantra,* 24 Sept. 1955, p. 36.
6. *The Realities of Fiction* (London: Macmillan, 1963), p. 31.
7. "The Lyric Short Story: The Sketch of a History," *Studies in Short Fiction,* 6:4 (Summer 1969), p. 443.
8. Rev. of "Rhapsody in Red" by Manjeri S. Isvaran, *Swatantra*, 17.7.1954, p. 34.
9. "The Lyric Short Story: The Sketch of a History," p. 444.
10. Rev. of "Lord Love Us" by William Samson, *Swatantra*, 30.4.1944, p. 33.
11. Introduction, *Naked Shingles*, p. v.
12. "Manjeri Isvaran's Stories," *The Hindu*, 29 January 1956, n.p.
13. Palgrave, Preface, *Golden Treasury of Songs and Lyrics* (London: Macmillan, 1959), p. vii.
14. *The Dimensions of Short Story: A Critical Anthology*, p. 510.
15. *The Dimensions of Short Story: A Critical Anthology*, p. 518.
16. *The Advantages of Lyric: Essays on Feeling in Poetry* (Bloomington: Indiana UP, 1977), p. 1.
17. Introduction, *The Art of Fiction* (New York: Holt, Rinehart and Winston, 1978), p. 4.
18. *Naked Shingles*, p. 89.
19. *Rickshawallah*, p. 79.
20. *Immersion*, p. 6.
21. "What Inspiration Feels Like," *Ten Modern Masters,* p. 533.
22. Isvaran, *The Writer* (Typescript).
23. "The Reading and Writing of Short Story," *The Atlantic Monthly* (February 1949), CLXXXIII, p. 56.
24. *No Ankletbells for Her*, p. 3.
25. *Naked Shingles*, pp. 27-28.
26. "Moonlight on a Broken Battle," *Ten Modern Masters,* p. 535.
27. *Aryan Path*, December 1957, p. 537.
28. *The Art of Modern Fictions* (New York: Rinehart, 1949), p. 3.
29. "Fiction at its highest," *Ten Modern Masters* p. 537.
30. *The Short Story* (London: Collin's, 1948), p. 138.
31. Rev. "The Hill of Devi" by E.M. Forster, *Swatantra*, December 1953, p. 30.
32. *The Art of Modern Fiction*, p. 3.

Technique and Style

The technique of narrating a story is determined by the kind of experience and the quality of vision which the author seeks to convey through the mutual interaction of character and plot. Works by eminent practitioners of the genre, however, bear testimony to the fact that the artistic value of a good story lies ultimately in something beyond method and technique. Kempton has rightly observed, "a noble theme may sound merely pretentious under poor telling."[1] Form and technique, it must be admitted, make the vital elements of the short story, for they are inseparable from the subject matter of the short story. To many readers, "the way of telling is the mark of good fiction: scene, detail, dialogue all the elements that make an imaginative creation of life."[2]

As a pioneer of Indian short story in English, Isvaran attempts a synthesis between the old and the new, and the Eastern and the Western methods of writing short fiction. Since the short story is the chosen literary genre of Isvaran, he experiments with the form and tries to understand the vital and varied principles of its composition. He "experiments with form and technique with a considerable degree of success."[3] Isvaran's stories, book-reviews, and literary essays, reveal his search for a consistent aesthetic. He maintains in his essay "Novelist as Artist": "Fiction when it is art, is the offspring of pure temperament and temperament is infinite in variety. And it is temperament that creates the technique and technique which stamps the artist. Fiction as art succeeds to the degree in which the temperaments of both writer and reader achieve harmony."[4] Isvaran is very much concerned with the technique of the short story and he has something very interesting to say about it.

Isvaran's acquaintance with the stories of the great masters of the art form makes him consider technique "as a tool box, an assortment of ways and means with all of which a writer should be familiar before he ponders the best way of telling a story."[5] His successful stories are chiselled pieces of literary workmanship and art. They are compact, neatly structured and remarkable for their finish. A careful exercise of strict self-restraint in order to achieve unity of impression makes these stories well-knit. He is careful in eliminating the superfluous details detrimental to the creation of the singleness of impression, though some of his stories are wrought with features that may be termed "loose," features, characteristic of the early practitioners of this genre in India. In the selection of incidents, and knitting them into stories of a high artistic order, Isvaran is supreme when viewed against contemporary standards of composition. Though Isvaran is familiar with the works of the great masters of the art, and has absorbed the best that he has come across in them, he has his own methods of telling a story. His technique at its best draws the reader very close to the emotional centre of the story so that the author, the reader and the leading characters all seem to be experiencing the same emotions. In his best stories, he eliminates everything that decelerates the emotional impact.

As a writer, very much taken up by the short story form, Isvaran knows that the short story with its obvious limitations cannot exhibit life in its entirety and multi-faceted complexity, for this needs a larger canvas than the story provides. We see characters in a short story only for a comparatively short span of time and see them circumscribed by a few relationships and limited circumstances. So he hardly attempts to entangle himself in the intricacies of plot and consciously veers away from complexity of structure and elaborate design which may complicate the interpretation of characters and of life.

The artistically successful stories of Isvaran reveal his belief that the significance of a work lies in the careful selection of its material. Isvaran's usual method is to select the salient details and then focus on a few exceptions to this wonted practice. He has an acute perception of the detail that he needs. In the details that he provides each word carries weight, laden as it is with layers of meaning.

Isvaran, who is aware of the limited scope of short fiction concentrates on a single situation and on one or two characters on whom is centred the dramatic situation which forms the climax of the story. Even when the requisites of the story demand the involvement of a number of characters, the focus is invariably on one or two. Even in the long story "Rickshawallah," that has all the potentialities and attributes of a novel, being "a photograph of life (rather than) a snapshot,"[6] the centre of attention is the honest Rickshawallah. As in a novel there are many characters in the story and inevitably so, as it deals with the life and death of the protagonist. However, these characters, except the protagonist, are merely functional creatures adding to the stature of the hero and contributing to the development of the plot. In "The Motorman," another of the long short soties of Isvaran, there are several characters but none overshadows the protagonist. "Immersion," which has been acclaimed to be Isvaran's magnum opus, has only four characters, but here also Akhileswaran and Jagadamma stand out as the leading figures. Thus, in matters relating to characters Isvaran sticks to the conventional norm, "short stories do frequently focus on one or two individuals who are seen as separated from their fellowmen in some way, at odds with the social norms, beyond the pale."[7]

Technically, a story tries to set up and maintain an illusion of life by recording a sequence of facts. This is achieved by the dramatic treatment of themes and by the pictorial clarity of the scene and action which produces a powerful dramatic appeal than by presenting a logical sequence of events. This method is perhaps most suited to present and project the character's states of mind without any authorial interference.

The most significant aspect of technique, viz. point of view, draws attention to the "relation in which the narrator stands to the story."[8] In the short story, more than in any other fictional form, the point of view is vital both as a device for the heightening of the dramatic tempo and, through the handling of the perspective upon the material, for the positive explanation and analysis of the theme.

Isvaran uses point of view to gain greater objectivity. In some of his stories he seeks it through self-effacement, by introducing a first-person narrator who is a participant in the action. In the stories which deal with serious themes, or reworks on ancient ones Isvaran adopts a point of view that is totally impersonal. As the 'acknowledged creator' he knows everything, but is no more than a witness to the action of the story. He does not adopt the point of view of either the focal characters or an omniscient observer in these stories. He is omnipresent, that is all. In "Immersion," "The Dance of Siva" "Sivaratri," "Revelation" and a number of other stories he is both omnipresent and omniscient. In these stories the author talks about the characters and about the story. He sees into the minds of the characters and chooses sometimes to report what they are thinking. In "Immersion" we hear the authorial voice as in the passage, "In his perch in the cart he was as happy as a king."[9] The following passage is another illustration of the omniscience of the author: "He was in such a fine frenzy of bliss that he wanted to catch the stars in the loop of his whipstring, pull them from the sky, and set them as jewels on rings for his fingers and the fingers of his beloved." (6-7) Again, "Akhileswaran's thoughts hovered round the pot, thoughts of profound worship and devotion, withal of great ache, of an endless sorrow." (12)

In "Revelation" Isvaran lays bare the mind of the young couple. "She dwelt pleasantly on the many sweet, secret things of him, of which she alone had the intimate knowledge."[10] In "No Ankletbells for Her" Isvaran not only reports, but freely offers comments on his role as the omniscient author: "Maybe she remembered vaguely, when she smiled, the painted eunuchs she had seen dancing before shop fronts during the pongal festival. No ballerina that pirouetted on a stage that changed under changing lights and shadows, with an auditorium bewitched before her starry eyes and the symphony of the orchestra falling divinely on her ears, no devadasi that did her natya in the temple in the presence of the decorated idol of god or goddess could have been so ecstatic as was this child of gutters." (3)

As a story-teller Isvaran knows naturally much more than what the characters in the story know. For example, he tells us of the unspoken thoughts of the priest in the story "Immersion" who cleverly guesses "what had happened" between the cartman and Jagada on hearing the last words of the cartman. Again, the attitude of the priest towards Akhileswaran on knowing this is not known to the protagonist but to the author. Omniscience of the author also permits him to delve into philosophic depths on what happens in the story. Isvaran's concept of beauty as manifest in Jagada illustrates this: "What is beauty and perfection in the eyes of man is not so to the creator who endowed such on an individual life; if it is destroyed in an unnatural way it cannot be said that an accident caused the destruction, it is the result of a sin the individual had committed in a previous existence. Beauty and perfection are only when God liberates that life from the bondage of birth."[11]

Isvaran's stories do not suffer from the major drawback of third-person omniscient point of view—distraction from the main issue of the story, the central character and his/her problem when the author concentrates on certain minor characters as the course of the story warrants. This is mainly because of the authorial preoccupation with one or two major characters.

Yet another point of view effectively experimented is that of making one of the characters narrate the story. This, he thinks, suits the immediacy of characters and actions. One of the disadvantages of this method is that of finding out a suitable place to fit the author in the story as the narrator. However, Isvaran's stories of this kind prove to be some of his best, but some others are technically failures. "The Man behind the Chair" is a successful story of this kind. The story begins with an account of the circumstances which make the narrator listen to the story of the protagonist. Though the introduction seems a little longer than is strictly necessary, once the reader begins to experience the tension in the story, the listener's (narrator's) response becomes vital. Here the dramatic situation and the tension are provided by the narrator and the protagonist, though several characters figure in the story. Though the narration centres round a series of misfortunes which should naturally arouse our pity for the protagonist, the reactions of the narrator at certain stages arouse feelings of humour and irony. "Toilette" depicts an aged husband's indifference to, or even ignorance of, the romantic longings of his young wife. The heart of the situation is revealed by the reflections of a witness to the whole drama. The presentation here is graphic. The narrator, who is also a passenger in the crowded third class railway compartment bound for Calcutta, does not philosophize or make any comment on what happens. But his reactions make a clue to large significance. In the stories "Annihilation," "Only a Sparrow," "That Moan," "A Bold Stroke" and "Strictly Professional," the narrator's role is only that of a witness. But the narrator is not characterized as illiterate or too ignorant to understand the full implications of the happenings. The philosophic musings on the apparently trivial incidents form the central elements in these stories. Each narrator is assigned the appropriate status to create the necessary credibility. Some of the episodes in the stories emphasize the mood and inner feelings and the appropriate nature attributed to the narrator.

The frame of reference for the short story is rarely the totality of a human life. An experienced artist, however, knows the appropriate point at which he can approach the story and the point selected determines the form. Isvaran observes: "Form need not always be the God of Gods in the short story—for every artist creates his own form—but such description inside its taut frame and texture swamp its purpose and the montage of multicoloured words while displaying glamour debilitates its energy. A novel has many mansions for such display, but the short story is a little room which cannot admit any redundancy."[12]

Isvaran experimented with a wide variety of approaches vis-a-vis the form of the short story. Apart from the third-person narration and the first-person narration, he has tried the autobiographical, reminiscential, flashback and one-sided personal correspondence. In "Painted Tigers" and "Gold on His Lips" the form of telling is autobiographical. He begins some of his stories in a slow, casual and leisurely manner as the narration in the stories "The Motorman," "A Madras Admiral" and "Painted Tigers" reveals. The long introductory passages betray this weakness of Isvaran's technique though it was a fashion of the day. Despite this, Isvaran could write technically perfect stories. The two stories "Consummation" and "Revelation" on identical theme and situation unravel the strength and weakness of Isvaran's technique. Both the stories are the revelation of the state of the mind of the ultra-sensitive husband on the first night. In both the stories the narrator is the omniscient author. In "Revelation" the story is narrated directly whereas in "Consummation" it is constructed from a one-sided correspondence made by the protagonist to a journal of which the narrator is the editor. "Consummation" begins in an "irritatingly" slow pace and lingers "to unfold for the reader the little incidentals and wayward episodes."[13] The narration of the circumstances which lead him to reconstruct the story from the pages of a journal itself takes as many as four pages. The conclusion is a letter received by the author from the protagonist, and it consists of about three full pages. The reader of the story has to grope for the 'single episode' that is the "heart of the story." The story is an illustration of how an effective theme of a good short story can be smothered under the combined burden of long drawn-out and rambling introduction, vague and diffuse presentation and a loquacious and dissipated ending. "Consummation" bears out the truth of M.K. Naik's charge, "His besetting sin is the irritatingly leisurely mode of narration he often indulges in, and his fatal habit of prolonging the story even after the point has been made."[14] On the other hand, "Revelation" consists only of six pages in which the theme is presented in a dramatic manner. It begins with a brief statement of the special reasons for the hilarity of Savitri who has been married for two years, on the third anniversary of their nuptial night. The whole atmosphere and background of the story are suggested in a short eloquent paragraph and the atmosphere which prevails throughout the story is in consonance with the tempo of this introductory paragraph. The scene of the first night of Savitri and Brihadisvaran is recalled from the point of view of the husband and wife. The embarrassing situation of the husband on the nuptial night and the bride pretending to be asleep and the final revelation of the secret to him, all are dramatized in the most effective manner. The story is considered to be one of the finest by Isvaran in its thematic unity, homogeneity of mood, clarity of tone, economy of narration, structural harmony and emotional richness.

Isvaran's descriptions of the personal appearance of his characters at times appear incongruous with the purpose of the story. At times they have no relevance to the theme or mood or tone of the story. The first three pages of the story "The Motorman" are devoted to describe the circumstances which lead the author to become interested in the story of the protagonist. This naturally mars the singleness of effect. Similarly "Tu Quoque" begins with a description of the beauty of a girl seen through the eye of a petty thief who, soon afterwards snatches the necklace of the girl. Anyway one can hardly associate a thief with the following passage:

> He saw her standing on the threshold of the house door opening on the street, a very pretty child about four years old, just a tiny bloom, windblown from a bloomy spray. She had eyes wide as

> wonder, and dark, dark abundant hair, too abundant for her age, plaited from the middle of the brow and joined to the braid curling petal-like at the nape. Child's innocence was her shining apparel, but her virgin shame was covered by a piece of beaten gold, fashioned like a little peepul leaf and swinging from a twisted alpaca thread tied about her waist. A necklace with a sovereign pendent was the only other ornament on her person and she stood on the threshold, opening and closing the door vigorously and delighted with the squealing of the hinges.[15]

In "Crutches," "Counsel for Defence" and "Silver Bead Golden Bead," a past incident is recapitulated by one of the characters. In "Between Two Flags," the form is that of a flashback in which the retired loyal bureaucrat R. Kalyan Rau Sastri recalls his past. In "Tu Quoque" the reader is taken directly into the story. In several of his stories, he does not follow the convention of ending a story in a passage that is characterized by brevity rather than loquacity. In them he continues putting down words after the solution has been reached, producing such an anti-climax that causes the loss of the effect that the beginning so richly promised.

In some of his stories Isvaran adopts a technique in which he integrates modern elements with those of folk-lore. In the individual and social life, he believes that the traditional culture and literature have infinite connotations. The story "The Miracle of the Door," a rework on a cultural lore, is written more like a fable than as a modern short story, a fable told by the narrator's grandmother who is a "first class raconteuse" whose story contains moral as bright as mirrors. In order to explain away things which are irrational the narrator says that it all happened when the grandmother was young. And now it seems to her "a dream, a shadow of superstition."[16] With its brevity, compression, dramatic touch and the focus on a moral, the story bears close resemblance to the fables of yore.

In all the stories of the collection *Fancy Tales*, Isvaran carefully balances nostalgic recollections with objectivity and judgement. Isvaran's contemporaries, by and large, have tried to relate their tales in some way or other to the great classics of India. Isvaran's method is to introduce into his story events that run to those in the ancient ages or juxtapose certain modern situations with those of the classics. Jagadamma, the major female character in "Immersion" is, as her name suggests, the mother of the universe and the archetype of Indian womanhood. In the *Ramayana,* Sita undergoes a series of sufferings for no fault of hers and is subjected to the process of purification by fire. Rama's life in the wilderness for fourteen years forms part of his sacred duty to enable his father keep his promise to the royal consort. 'Akhileswaran' means 'the Lord of the universe' and the Akhileswaran of the story is bound with his 'sacred duty to his father.'

Apart from drawing characters and situations parallel to those in antiquity, Isvaran refers to episodes in Indian classics to evolve a sense of deeper perception. The helpless Jagada before the satiric cartman is compared to Draupadi in a similar situation, a situation that ultimately leads to the annihilation of a whole dynasty. "Where was He Whom Draupadi invoked in the darkest hour of her shame and grief, Who came to succour her? Perhaps the present situation was not tragic enough to deserve His attention, His glance of compassion; perhaps He regarded what He said, that to destroy the wicked, to protect the good and establish dharma He was born from age to age."[17]

In "Immersion," Isvaran utilizes myth to give a concrete shape to the abstract thought of Akhileswaran. The stories "Sivaratri," "The Dance of Siva" and "At His Nativity" are studded with mythical parallels and references as well as legendary tales to such an extent that any average reader is apt to be struck by the contemporary relevance of our classics. It becomes imperative for a reader to share the myths with the story-teller for a thorough comprehension. Though frequent references are made to local myths, they are explicit enough to be easily comprehensible to the reader.

As the tone of a story is inseparable from style, so style is inseparable from the meaning that it attempts to convey. The voice of the artist emerges from the very vibration of his prose—the stylistic devices which initiate the reader into an awareness of the contrived significance. So any investigation into the stories of Isvaran will be incomplete without a study of his prose style in relation to tone, mood and atmosphere, for "the words used by the tale teller were as the colours used by the painter or the clothes of the tale."[18]

Isvaran's theories on the art of short fiction, that lie spread over various literary pieces and reviews reveal that he has made ardent efforts to cultivate a graceful and elegant style. However, there seems to be no strain involved in those efforts and no pain is manifest in his attempt to be brilliant and effective. About his own efforts to achieve stylistic perfection, he observes, "Every story or poem I wrote I destroyed three, often six and got my hand steady, stiffening myself the while within, not to inflict any piece I considered feeble on others."[19] It has to be acknowledged in this connection that a great master of the short story genre has done similar things, to achieve perfect style and craftsmanship. While reviewing the book *The Stories of Frank O'-*

Connor, Isvaran quotes O'Connor's words: "Some of the stories had already been re-written twenty, thirty, even fifty times."[20]

In bringing the language under perfect control to suit the tone and theme, Isvaran has achieved a success that is comparable to that of the great master of the art form. His language is simple, lucid and effective without being deliberate or laboured. In giving forth the tone by means of the texture of his prose and by the verbal resonance of the recorded event, Isvaran's attainment is remarkable. The authorial voice reveals itself from the very vibration of his prose. The structure of "Jowramma" consists of a series of shifting moods of agreement and disagreement. The meaning of the story is formed by the structure of contrasted moods. The description of nature becomes eminently symbolic of the changing pattern of the relationship of the village girl Jowramma and her husband. Their life is temporarily shrouded in misery by the fog of disagreement and finally the shadow is cleared by the light of conjugal pleasure that has hitherto characterized their life. The changing patterns of fog and sunlight are represented symbolically in the very rhythm of the prose. Here is a passage, for instance:

> The day had begun clear and bright but before moon the sun fell; shadows raced like steeds, dimpled in rings, and dissolved in hillslope, meadow, and valley; from beyond the greys and quiet greens of silver oaks and eucalypti a mist, thin as muslin rose and moved on gathering speed and thickness. Soon the countryside was in a huge cloudage of fog; heaven and earth had blended in radiant obscurity.
>
> From somewhere a sound came startling the silence; it swelled, it was the electric horn mooing the hour of twelve. The fog which had begun to lift a while ago cleared away completely when the mooing ceased; church steeples tapered into the sky again; and treetops shed their opals enriching every dip and dingle, every hole and hummock in the earth; and meadows lay freshened and humming in their emeraldness.[21]

The purpose of the artist at the beginning of the story "The Miracle of the Door" is to make the reader believe something unbelievable. The primary device used is to show the distance between the date of the actual happening and the narrator-spectator's retelling the tale. It becomes a thrice-told tale. The purpose of the writer then becomes that of creating a mysterious atmosphere built out of the setting, located vaguely as 'long ago' and by a chain of supernatural incidents.

Sean O'Faolain remarks that a writer, at the very opening, "must make an immediate and intimate contact with his story." He further observes, "For this reason, I confess, I tend to judge most of the stories I read by the opening sentences."[22] If judged on the basis of the standards set by O'Faolain, the beginning of a story like "The Painted Tigers" or "The Motorman" or "Mythili" is guilty of being slow and leisurely, setting the scene and giving us information which has no direct bearing on the core of the tale. What we recognize as crucially important is often distanced. The descriptions given at the beginning of these stories are quite irrelevant in a good short story for these descriptions are general and vague and an ideal short story cannot afford to be vague or general at any point. The beginning should be direct and to the point, like that of stories like "Tu Quoque" "Kolu" or "The Cradle."

However, the clarity of Isvaran's mind can do anything that is required by the context—modulate the trivial into the momentous, the prosaic into the eloquent, without ever losing the poise and authority of aesthetics. "As a stylist he has an unerring ear for the right word in the right place, which can neither be translated nor transposed. His word-music casts a spell. The finest nuances are at his command. He is something of a word-juggler too, and the rarest expression, if it is the aptest, is to be found in his bag of verbal tricks. But he hates to revel in mere bombast or wallow in empty rhetoric. Nor does he like to indulge in obscurity for obscurity's sake."[23] It is also noteworthy that the meaning of narration in his best stories is carried to some extent by pitch and syntactical arrangement.

A study of the style of a creative writer who opts for a language other than his mother tongue must examine the extent to which his language is conditioned by his socio-cultural background and the linguistic feature of his mother tongue. It becomes natural for such a writer to exploit various linguistic devices to develop a medium that fully suits the needs of expressing his thoughts and sensibilities. This will inevitably make the language different from the variety of the language used by the native speakers of it. The variations are manifest at various linguistic levels—lexical, syntactic and semantic, apart from the idiosyncratic features of his use of the language.

At the lexical level, Isvaran has drawn a number of words from myths, scriptures, classical literature, and folk-tales, in addition to the names of characters and places which are Indian. Words like 'upanayana,' 'dharma,' 'Karma,' 'Saptapadi,' bairagee,' 'shradha,' 'kolu' etc. have spiritual and philosophical connotations. These words have no exact equivalents in English.

Expressions like 'Exit from this world,' 'Sacred Vigil,' 'Married with Agni as witness' are all alien to the native variety of English. The use of proverbs like "eating goose berry tastes sour at first but which a draught of water makes sweet," "After all, every God-created thing, however small has a belly to fill" and "as a drop in the ocean" is another significant aspect of his diction. Images like "bearing the figure of Goddess Lakshmi rising from the full-blown lotus," "The doors of the temple shut and no lamp burns," "flowers of yesterday lie festering" require for full comprehension, a knowledge of Indian background.

At the syntactic level, a marked feature of Isvaran's style is the use of complex sentences which result in large scale embedding. This feature was common in Tamil and Malayalam in the forties and fifties. However, it must be noticed that, apart from these inevitable features of mother tongue interference, Isvaran's English carries the essential features of "chaste British English."

NOTES

1. Kenneth Payson Kempton, *The Short Story* (Cambridge: Harvard UP, 1954), p. 33.
2. *The Dimensions of the Short Story: A Critical Anthology*, p. 514.
3. John Hampson, Introduction, *No Ankletbells for Her*, p. xv.
4. *Swatantra*, 9 January 1954, p. 31.
5. Kenneth Payson Kempton, p. 33.
6. Sunilkumar Bose, rev. *Rickshawallah, Modern Review*, 6 Sept. 1947, p. 37.
7. Ian Reid, *The Short Story*, p. 27.
8. Percy Lubbock, *The Craft of Fiction*, (London: Jonathan Cape, 1965), p. 251.
9. *Immersion*, pp. 4-5.
10. *No Ankletbells for Her*, p. 26.
11. *Immersion*, p. 48.
12. Isvaran, rev. "White Wand and Other Stories" by L.P. Hartley, *Swatantra*, 18 December 1954, p. 33.
13. Valerie Shaw, *Short Story: A Critical Introduction*, p. 46.
14. *A History of Indian English Literature*, p. 80.
15. *Naked Shingles*, pp. 74-75.
16. *Angry Dust*, pp. 12.
17. *Immersion*, pp. 47-48.
18. *The Dimensions of the Short Story: A Critical Anthology*, p. 523.
19. "The Indian Writer in English," p. 10.
20. *Swatantra*, 23 Jan. 1954, p. 34.
21. *Naked Shingles* pp. 16-17.
22. *The Short Story* (London: Collins, 1948), p. 192.
23. D. Anjaneyulu, *Thought*, 10 Aug. 1963, n.p.

Conclusion

Isvaran is the first Indian English writer of irrefutable creative force and distinguished literary talent to accept the short story as his artistic medium at a time when it held forth few challenges and few takers in the land. He is the only Indian writer in English to establish a reputation mainly on the basis of his achievement as a short story writer, though one can hardly ignore his substantial contribution to Indian poetry in English.

Throughout Isvaran's literary career he was concerned with the investigation of the aesthetics of the short story as a literary genre and experimented with different modes of its composition. While reviewing the short stories of the great Western exponents of the form, he got to know the thematic and technical factors that contributed substantially to make them great and effective masters of the art form. As literary models, writers like Edgar Allen Poe, Chekhov, Katherine Mansfield, Joseph Conrad, A.E. Coppard, Frank O'Connor H.E. Bates and Henry James exercised considerable influence on Isvaran. In his growth as a writer of short stories, Isvaran was profoundly influenced in his method by the American writers who were "breaking away from tradition and opening unexpected horizons to set life against, with deliberate speed, majestic instancy."[1] Aware as he was of the origin of the modern short story in primitive forms like fables, parables, folk tales, fairy stories, rituals and later developments like scriptures and epics, he modelled his own tales on them.

The characteristic features of Poe's stories, like the creation of portentous atmosphere, melancholy forebodings, learned allusions and careful use of stylistic devices to create lyrical effect—all find their echoes in the serious tales of Isvaran. He acknowledges the American influence when he writes: "American authors like Benjamin Appeal, William Faulkner, William Saroyan and Ernest Hemingway are in the vanguard, while those like Dorothy McCleary, Morley Callaghan and Louis Hamet who bring up the rear are equally fine craftsmen in the field." (vi) To Isvaran, Chekhov "is the supreme master of the short stories." (vi) In the words of Isvaran, Chekhov's short stories represent a "new type of journey into the interior of Russian mind." (vi) This must have inspired Isvaran to undertake his journeys into the Indian sensibility. In order to do so, he singles out decisive or crucial moments in the life of his character rather than sail with the tide of life. His manner of unfolding the inner man has a Chekhovian touch about it. At the same time, the reader is made to feel that the totality of life is there behind the slice that is presented in the story. There are moments in the lives of all, which, in a flash, reveal the larger significance of a whole life-time. Like Chekhov Isvaran creates his characters in such a way that their inward reality is directly accessible to the readers. In the typical Chekhovian manner, Isvaran avoids describing the psychological state of his characters. It is made, in most cases, manifest in their actions.

Isvaran was also indebted to Russian geniuses like Turgenev, Tolstoy, Gogol, Dostoevsky and Gorky, but the most potent of the Russian influences was that of Chekhov. Katherine Mansfield and A.E. Coppard too, who liberated the English short story "from the slavery of prosaic dullness, heavily loaded metaphors, morbid sluggishness, adult infantilism and romantic fantasy,"[2] influenced Isvaran to a considerable extent. They have been acknowledged to be the artists who "distilled into the form of the English short story the quintessence of lyricism."[3] Both the writers have imbibed Russian influence in their literary works. The influence of these writers has been instrumental, among other things, in making Isvaran's stories lyrical.

Isvaran is anxious to give due consideration to man's sentiments, to his subjective life, for he seems to be convinced that man's passionate life is more significant than the objective world—a literary approach perfected by Mansfield and Coppard. Like Katherine Mansfield, Isvaran is at his best in depicting the feminine world.

It should, however, be borne in mind that Isvaran did not follow slavishly those whom he emulated. He held that Mansfield was not in any way profound but admired her for the clarity of her mind and directness of thinking. But Coppard's was the "biggest achievement in the field." (ix) According to Isvaran, Coppard is "an author's author" and "his portrait gallery is rich and marvellous, luminous with all the strata of light." (ix) As in the case of Coppard, the deceptive simplicity of Isvaran's stories conceals a widely admired technical skill. Many of the most characteristic of his tales have rural or suburban setting and display a deep sympathy for the odd and the misfit. Isvaran indicates to what extent he was influenced by his predecessors and contemporaries in the field: "In the republic of letters it is hard for contemporaries to escape the influence of one another. From models and modes, through the maturing stages of deflected thought and craftsmanship is the individual personality born." (x)

Of all the oldest and the most enduring of Indian literary forms, those that influenced Isvaran most were the folk tales, fables and parables. Many of his stories that have first-person narrators, bear the characteristics of oral tradition. Few of his realistic stories are without moralistic overtones. By reason of brevity they are endowed with an intensity of style as well as of vision.

As in a fable the incidents in his stories are presented for the meaning they carry. Apart from these, the Indian classics and scriptures as also the social and political, economic and religious, moral and cultural forces at work during his time exercised a powerful influence in shaping his literary career. His gifts as a story-teller and poet are remarkably strong and definite. It seems that he was guided by a strong conviction that the first duty of an artist is to master his instrument. So, he tried to make his own all that was best in the acknowledged practitioners of the genre. Despite the manifold influences which played a profound role in the shaping of the particular kind of literary construction he had chosen, Isvaran remains essentially an Indian in his vision of life and art. His work emerges from and revolves round an intense moral awareness of the national movement which his contemporaries had chosen as their major concern.

C.V. Venugopal, who has made an in-depth study of Indian short story in English, considers Isvaran one of the four major writers of short fiction in English, the others being Raja Rao, Mulk Raj Anand and R.K. Narayan. He observes, "all these four writers have spelt out in no uncertain terms their conceptions of short story as a form—conceptions which have guided their own practice."[4] They portray the social scene in India in their tales though their approaches are determined by their personal predilections. While Isvaran is primarily concerned with a search for the significant truths underlying human relationship, Anand creates in his readers an awareness of the social evils, that may provoke them into launching a movement to establish a new social order, devoid of economic exploitation and social degradation brought about by evils like untouchability. Raja Rao is primarily concerned with the creation of myths by idealizing his characters. R.K. Narayan's concern is with the middle-class people of a little town he has created. His approach is realistic rather than reformative.

Isvaran sees religion as a means by which the individual acquires his moral virtues. Religious observances effect the moral upliftment of the individual. To Anand religion is a perpetuator of social evils like untouchability, casteism, superstition and exploitation, and hence a pernicious force. On the other hand, Raja Rao portrays the spiritual and metaphysical aspects of religion. His characters have firm faith in God who invests their lives with a larger significance. R.K. Narayan's fictional world is predominantly a Hindu world but he avoids religious themes just as he avoids political themes. His approach is that of social realism. His capabilities lie primarily in drawing upon the sanctions of traditional Indian morality. In his moral and religious concept, Isvaran is closer to R.K. Narayan than to Mulk Raj Anand and Raja Rao.

Isvaran had his literary apprenticeship as "a humble worker in the medium" by launching a magazine called *The Short Story* aimed at the promotion of the genre. He grew into maturity as a writer, wrote "essays serious and frivolous, short stories which turned out to be sketches which unfolded into stories, playlets, film scripts and plenty of book reviews." (xi)

The seventy-odd short stories Isvaran wrote entitle him to the rank of a talented practitioner of the then nascent literary form. Some of these stories are short and some very long. Some deal with domestic life and some with social relations while some are endowed with spiritual overtones and some others are packed with action. Some merely express a mood, some deal with a single episode, some narrate a series of them.

In theme and characterization, Isvaran displays remarkably rich variety. His portrait gallery includes farmers, drivers, rickshaw-pullers, bureaucrats, office peons, soldiers, lawyers, landlords, police officers, priests, children, widows, thieves, barbers, hawkers, morons, pious and wise grandmothers, townsfolk of middle and lower class and slum-dwellers—all take their substance and meaning from the reality of Indian life. The setting and way of telling the tale remain authentically Indian and hence his objective detachment from his theme and his characters. As a story-teller, he has unquestioned faith in the validity and contemporary relevance of all that is best in the long tradition of Indian literature and culture. Facts and figures that feature in his fictional world form the warp and woof of the complex fabric of Indian tradition. Religion and imagination form an integral part of this tradition. As a result, Isvaran's literary imagination is inseparable from his thoughts about the transcendent.

The Indian literary tradition is manifest in all the stories of Isvaran. The social, religious and political atmosphere of that part of the country where he was born and brought up—its beliefs, superstitions, rituals, customs and traditions—have shaped his sensibility and attitude to life. The vision of life and the Indian sensibility formulated by the early influence have been little affected by his later exposure to a Western system of education and his contact with a galaxy of eminent men of letters of the West and his acceptance of a literary form evolved and perfected in America, Russia, France and England. The unique Indian atmosphere informs the fictional and poetic worlds of Isvaran. They epitomize a distinctive Indian sensibility expressed in English language.

The locale of Isvaran's stories is typically South Indian whereas his major characters are moulded in the matrix conceived in the great classics of India. These characters are culturally and emotionally rooted in the family. Most of his stories deal with human behaviour in the familial context. His values operate within the parameters set by the family as conceptualized by Indian tradition.

Isvaran's fictional world is predominantly a Hindu world in which religion plays an over-riding role in the individual, familial, social, cultural and spiritual life of its members. The three major stories "Immersion," "Sivaratri," and "The Dance of Siva" have religious observances and rituals as their major concern. "Immersion" deals mainly with rituals associated with marriage, child-birth, upanayana and funeral as also with those meant for the smooth transition of the soul from here to the hereafter. The life of a true Hindu in its totality is conceived in these stories. "Sivaratri" explores the ritualistic tradition that Hinduism has so steadfastly followed through generations. The temporal range and relevance of the tradition are suggested through the narration of the spiritualistic experiences of three distinct groups of people. "The Dance of Siva" presents the unique vision of the author that determines his concept of art that in its pristine character was a form of religious worship. A spiritual experience that is peculiarly Indian forms the major episode in the story.

Isvaran's stories like "Naked Shingles," "Mango Lane," "Crutches," "The Last Pawn" "The Painted Tigers," "Rickshawallah," "Strictly Professional," "Counsel for Defence" and "That Moan" mark his firmer grasp of the socio-economic conditions of his time and a deeper understanding of the human nature. These stories present a realistic picture of the countryside or suburban areas of south India, with its illiteracy, ignorance, superstition, inertia, petty jealousy, hatred and pride. They have not only a philosophic dimension but a humanistic touch.

The events that make up stories like "Mythili," "Revelation" and "Saturday is Saturday" are not of any major import. These stories are mere recitals of trivial experiences felt by his characters. In contrast to these stories that deal with banal incidents of everyday life in a lighter vein, stories like "Consummation," "A Light Was Lit," "Passage Money," "Overwrought" and "No Birds Sing" present the grim aspects of life. The mental disposition of his characters in these stories is responsible for their misfortunes and of others who come into contact with them. These stories delineate the mind's construction manifest in human responses and reactions on a variety of occasions.

The place of women in the family and the misery meted out to them by man, knowingly or unknowingly, forms a major theme of many of his stories. "Merry Go Round," "Jowramma," "Sea Shells," "Mythili," "The Motorman," "Sympathy" and a few other stories deal with this overtly or covertly.

Isvaran depicts children in their manifold relationships either in the family or in the society in half a dozen stories. These stories reveal his intimate knowledge of the mental mechanics of children belonging to the middle class or lower class. "No Ankletbells for Her," "Kolu," "Beginnings," "Death of a Doll," "Justice" and "A Gap in the Wall" bear testimony to Isvaran's knowledge of child psychology and his empathic capabilities.

The stories "Posthumous Award," "The War Memorial" and "Peaceful was the Night" portray three distinct faces of war—the bereavement of aged parents, the meaninglessness of gallantry awards and the pity of war.

A few of Isvaran's stories are concerned with contemporary social realities and are delineations of certain actual incidents in the life of the author. These stories are endowed with his characteristic warmth and intensity of feeling. They are mostly set in motion by some reverie of nostalgic harking back to the past. "Angry Dust" and "Gold on His Lips" depict actual experiences of the author. "The Cradle," "The Miracle of the Door," "At his Nativity," "Sea Shells" and "Sivaratri" echo tales of the oral tradition wrapped in some religious superstition or social morality. Other stories are modelled after fairy tales or fables. "Thoughtless Donkey," "The Serpent Gem" and "Illumination" resemble traditional Indian animal fables. "Bewitched," "A Bold Stroke" and "Illumination" combine the qualities of traditional folklore and the shapely modern short story. All the stories in the collection *Fancy Tales* are fairy tales meant for children and the grown-ups alike. Plots of stories like "The Man behind the Chair" and "Toilette" are nightmares and dreams.

In form and technique Isvaran's stories present an amalgam of the methods employed in the fable, the parable, the epic, the folk-tales and the modern shapely short story. Each story tries to explore the varied possibilities of telling a tale and out of the models he has examined, he evolves a method suited to his theme. He has a superb perception of the details that he needs for each story and each word that he uses has its connotative as well as denotative relevance. As for characterization, he concentrates on one or two characters. He maintains an illusion of life by the dramatic treatment of themes and by the graphic presentation of scenes and actions.

Isvaran's choice of fictional perspectives varies from one type of stories to another. In stories dealing with serious aspects of life or religious themes, impersonal narration is used. In them the author is the omniscient, third-person narrator. In a few works, the story is narrated by one of the characters, though the authorial presence in such tales is more or less apparent. Yet another point of view that he has successfully employed is that of the narrator as a mute witness. Whatever may be the assigned status of the narrator, he is presented in such a way that his credibility is never in question.

Besides, Isvaran has successfully experimented with autobiographical, reminiscential, flashback and one-sided personal correspondence. He seldom loses an opportunity to relate his tales to the classics of India. He places characters and situations from the classics in the modern context, thereby concretizing his abstract visions. His stories are replete with references to folk-lore and local myths.

All through his career as a short-story writer, Isvaran has been concerned with the mastering of a perfect system to communicate his conceptions. He has succeeded in evolving a language that is simple, lucid and effective without being deliberate or laboured. His prose style is quite in keeping with the tone that he has set for each story.

Isvaran's stories, more often than not, approximate the lyric. His acquisition of a personal idiom and a maturity of expression in poetry before entering the world of story-tellers, enables him to examine the form in relation to other literary genres, especially lyrics and import certain aesthetic forms of them into his short stories. Intense concentration and eloquent suggestiveness, lucidity of diction and reticence of expression that mark out a good lyric are characteristic of his stories, that are charged as much with keenness of feeling as with sensuousness. Isvaran's fictional world while portraying life from mythical times to his contemporary world even trespasses into the future. His concerns stretch from the remote past of the vedic period through the Indian national movement to the post-independence times.

What is peculiar about Indian culture, life and experience is that they do not easily admit of translation into a language alien to its culture. Isvaran wields the English language with the felicity and force of a native. His strength as a story-teller lies primarily in the mastery of the medium. The Indian complexion invariably shines through the English garb. Isvaran is, perhaps, the only Indian writer in English of the colonial period who has chosen an ancient medium and a foreign language to render indigenous life and experience and speech that have always defied artistic recreation in the past. K.S. Venkataramani has rightly observed, "there is no copper at all in the Manjeri marketplace."[5]

NOTES

1. Isvaran, "Something of Others and Myself," Introduction, *Rickshawallah*, p. 6.
2. Nariman Hormsaji, *Katherine Mansfield: An Appraisal* (London: Collins, 1967), p. 103.
3. *Ibid.*, pp. 103-4.
4. *Perspectives on Indian Fiction in English*, p. 225.
5. Introduction, *Naked Shingles*, p. 8.

Bibliography

Primary Sources

A. Fiction

Naked Shingles. Madras: Chitrabhanu, 1941.
Sivaratri. Madras: Huxley, 1943.
Angry Dust. Madras: Saktikaryalayam, 1944.
Rickshawallah. Madras: Alliance, 1946.
Fancy Tales. Madras: Saktikaryalayam, 1947.
No Ankletbells for Her. Madras: Mitra, 1949.
Immersion. Madras: S. Viswanathan, 1951.
Painted Tigers. Madras: Dhanus, 1956.
A Madras Admiral. Madras: Dhanus, 1959.
A Stillness at Sunset (unpublished).
Lustral Bath (unpublished).

B. Poetry

Saffron and Gold and Other Poems. Madras: The People's Printing and Publishing House, 1932.
Altar of Flowers. Oxford: Basil Blackwell, 1934.
Brief Orisons. Madras: Huxley, 1942.
The Fourth Avtar. Madras: Shaktikaryalayam, 1946.
Oblivion. Madras: Mitra, 1954.
The Neem is a Lady and Other Poems. Madras: Dhanus, 1957.
Sinning Heaven and Other Poems. Bareilly: Prakash, 1984.

C. Drama

Song of the Gipsymaiden. Madras: Saktikaryalayam, 1945.
Yama and Yami. Madras: S. Viswanathan, 1948.

D. Criticism

Venkataramani:Writer and Thinker: An Appreciation. Madras: The People's Printing and Publishing House, 1932.

E. Essays

"Tabloid Wisdom." *Swatantra*, 22 Aug. 1953:25-26.
"Indian Writing." *Swatantra*, 19 Sept. 1953:30-33.
"The Novelist as Artist." *Swatantra*, 9 Jan. 1954:30-32.
"Maugham Eetat Eight." *Swatantra*, 23 Jan. 1954:27.
"Bull Chasing." *Swatantra*, 27 Feb. 1954:31-33.
"Wordsworth: His 'Prelude' and the Upanishads." *Swatantara*, 10 April 1954:29-32.

"I Meet a Poet." *Swatantra*, 27 Aug. 1955:n.p.
"The Writer's Profession." *Swarajya*, 6 Oct. 1956:13.
"Raid on the Inarticulate." *Swarajya*, 27 Oct. 1956:8-9.
"Learning the Craft: Lessons from the Masters." *Swarajya*, 10 Nov. 1956:6+.
"Tapestry of Life: Criticism for Improvement." *Swarajya*, 6 July 1957:11+.
"The Indian Writer in English." *Swarajya* 21 Sept. 1957:10+.
"The Role of the Story Teller in the Modern World." *The Aryan Path*, Dec. 1957:535-38.
"John Hampson: A Portrait and a Study." *Triveni*, Jan. 1957:280-89.

F. Unpublished Essays

"The Art and Craft of Translation." ts.
"Book Reviews." ts.
"Book review in English." ts.
"M. Chalapati Rau." ts.
"The Creative Process." ts.
"Exchange of Regional Literatures." MS.
"He was of the Aristocracy of the Sensitive." ts.
"I believe." ts.
"The Illusion Called Socialism." ts.
"I came to Delhi" in the Series 'the First time,' ts.
"The Ideal Publisher." ts.
"Karl Shapiro." ts.
"On Translation." ts.
"The Peasant His Lot." ts.
"A Silence Explained." MS.
"Sociological Thought and Literature: Frontiers of Sociological Criticism." ts.
"Two Creative Artists." ts.
"VA. RA." ts.
"What is a Novel." ts.
"World Writing, A Conspectus with Special Reference to Indian Drama." ts.
"The Writer." ts.
"The Writer and the Public." ts.

G. Book Reviews

Rev. of *New World Writings: First and Second Mentor Selections*, ed. The New American Library of World Literature. *Swatantra*, 13 June 1953:29+.
"Ernest Hemingway: The Novelist as Artist." Rev. of the novels of Ernest Hemingway. *Swatantra*, 27 June 1953:33-34.
Rev. of *Lions and Shadows: An Education in the Twenties* by Christopher Isherwood. *Swatantra*, 25 July 1953:26+.
Rev. of *Perspectives*, Spring 1953. *Swatantra*, 1 Aug. 1953:36+.
Rev. of *Forrest Reid: A Portrait and a Study* by Russel Burlingham. *Swatantra*, 8 Aug. 1953:26-27.
Rev. of *Marshlands and Prometheus Unbound* by Andrew Gide. *Swatantra*, 22 Aug. 1953:28-30.
Rev. of *The Echoing Grove* by Rosamond Lehmann. *Swatahtra*, 22 Aug. 1953:30.
Rev. of *George Orwell* by Tom Hopkinson. *Swatantra*, 12 Sept. 1953:24-25.
Rev. of *Kingfishers Catch Fire* by Rumer Godden. *Swatantra*, 19 Sept. 1958:24-26.
Rev. of *An American Dream Girl* by James T. Farrel. *Swatantra*, 12 Sept. 1953:25.
Rev. of *Barabbas* by Par Lagerkvist. *Swatantra*, 26 Sept. 1953:39-40.

Rev. of *John Galsworthy* by R.M. Mottram. *Swatantra*, 3 Oct. 1953:34+.
Rev. of *Mythology* by Edith Hamilton. *Swatantra*, 10 Oct. 1953:35.
Rev. of *H.G. Wells* by Montgomery Belgion. *Swatantra*, 10 Oct. 1953:33-34.
Rev. of *The Other Place* by J.B. Priestly. *Swatantra*, 17 Oct. 1953:26+.
Rev. of *The Doctor and the Devils* by Dylan Thomas. *Swatantra*, 24 Oct. 1953:30+.
Rev. of *Poems 1953*, ed. Robert Groves. *Swatantra*, 31 Oct. 1953:27-29.
Rev. of *The Caravan Passes* by George Tabori. *Swatantra*, 31 Oct. 1953:29.
Rev. of *Encounter*, Vol. 1, No. 1, Oct. 1953. *Swatantra*, 14 Nov. 1953:35.
Rev. of *Humanities* by Desmond MacCarthy, *Swatantra*, 21 Nov. 1953:33-34.
Rev. of *Collected Stories* by Osbert Sitwell. *Swatantra*, 28 Nov. 1953:26-29.
Rev. of *The Rime of Indifference* by Alberto Moravia. *Swatantra*, 28 Nov. 1953:29.
Rev. of *The Hill of Devi: Being Letters from Devas State Senior* by E.M. Forster. *Swatantra*, 5 Dec. 1953:27-29.
Rev. of *The Writers Trade* by L.A.G. Strong. *Swatantra*, 12 Dec. 1953:29+.
Rev. of *Publish and be Damned: The Astonishing Story of the Daily Mirror* by Hugh Cudlipp. *Swatantra*, 19 Dec. 1953:41-43.
Rev. of *The Woman in the Case and Other Stories* by Anton Chekhov. *Swatantra*, 9 Jan. 1954:33-35.
Rev. of *The Stories of Frank O'Connor* by Frank O'Connor. *Swatantra*, 23 Jan. 1954:33-35.
Rev. of *Untouchable and Coolie* by Mulk Raj Anand. *Swatantra*, 23 Jan. 1954:35.
Rev. of *A Writer's Diary: Being Extracts from the Diary of Virginia Woolf*, ed. Leonard Woolf. *Swatantra*, 30 Jan. 1954:35-38.
Rev. of *In the Shadow of the Mahatma: A Personal Memoir* by G.D. Birla. *Swatantra*, 27 Feb. 1954:34.
Rev. of *Conversations with Kafka* by Gustav Janouh. *Swatantra*, 27 March 1954:29-31.
Rev. of *Phoenix Fled and Other Stories* by Attia Hosain. *Swatantra*, 27 March 1954:32.
Rev. of *The London Magazine*, ed. John Lehmann, Vol. 1, No. 1. Feb. 1954. *Swatantra*, 3 April 1954:27-30.
Rev. of *The Door of Perception* by Aldous Huxley. *Swatantra*, 24 April 1954:34-35.
Rev. of *Under Milk Wood: A Play for Voices* by Dylan Thomas. *Swatantra*, 22 May 1954:36+.
Rev. of *The City and the Wave* by Jon Godden. *Swatantra*, 29 May 1954:34-38.
Rev. of *A Charm against the Toothache* by John Heath-stubbs. *Swatantra*, 5 June 1954:34-36.
Rev. of *Bitter Honeymoon and Other Stories* by Alberto Moravia. *Swatantra*, 31 July 1954:34-35.
Rev. of *Gigi and Julie de Carneilhan* by Colette. *Swatantra*, 31 July 1954:35+.
Rev. of *Smoke Bellow* by Jack London. *Swatantra*, 31 July 1954:35+.
Rev. of *The World in the Evening* by Christopher Isherwood. *Swatantra*, 4 Sept. 1954:33-34.
Rev. of *A Spring Journey* by James Kirkup. *Swatantra*, 11 Sept. 1954:37-39.
Rev. of *Nightmares of Eminent Persons* by Bertrand Russell. *Swatantra*, 25 Sept. 1954:34-35.
Rev. of *England Your England and Other Essays* by George Orwell. *Swatantra*, 9 Oct. 1954:33-34.
Rev. of *Poems of Change* by Irene Coates. *Swatantra*, 16 Oct. 1954:35-36.
Rev. of *The Dance in India* by Faubion Bowers. *Swatantra*, 30 Oct. 1954:33.
Rev. of *Yield to the Night* by Joan Henry. *Swatantra*, 6 No. 1954:38+.
Rev. of *Soldiers Bathing and Other Poems* by F.T. Prince. *Swatantra*, 27 Nov. 1954:34-36.
Rev. of *The London Magazine*, Vol. 1, No. 10 Nov. 1954. *Swatantra*, 11 Dec. 1954:34-35.
Rev. of *The White Wand and Other Stories* by L.P. Hartley. *Swatantra*, 18 Dec. 1954:33-34.
Rev. of *The Black Swan* by Thomas Mann. *Swatantra*, 25 Dec. 1954:33-35.
Rev. of *William Shakespeare* by John Masefield. *Swatantra*, 8 Jan. 1955:33-34.

Rev. of *The Laughing Matter* by William Saroyan. *Swatantra*, 22 Jan. 1955:35-36.
Rev. of *Quite Early One Morning* by Dylan Thomas. *Swatantra*, 5 Feb. 1955:37-39.
Rev. of *A Few Late Chrysanthemums* by John Betjeman. *Swatantra*, 19 Feb. 1955:34-36.
Rev. of *Last Recollections of My Uncle Charles* by Nigel Balchin. *Swatantra*, 26 Feb. 1955:34-36.
Rev. of *Dead Man in the Silver Market: An Autobiographical Essay on National Pride* by Aubrey Menen. *Swatantra*, 5 March 1955: 35-37.
Rev. of *A Vision of Beasts and Gods* by George Barker. *Swatantra*, 19 March 1955:33-35.
Rev. of *Flesh and Blood* by Francis Mauriac. *Swatantra*, 26 March 1955:36+.
Rev. of *A World of Love* by Elizabeth Bowen. *Swatantra*, 9 April 1955:32-33.
Rev. of *A Ghost at Noon* by Alberto Moraviac. *Swatantra*, 23 April 1955:28-29.
Rev. of *Pope* by Ian Jack. *Swatantra*, 23 April 1955: 29-30.
Rev. of *Lord Love Us* by William Samson. *Swatantra*, 30 April 1955:33+.
Rev. of *Loser Takes All* by Graham Greene. *Swatantra*, 14 May 1955:35-36.
Rev. of *Homer's Daughter* by Robert Graves. *Swatantra*, 4 June 1955:33-35.
Rev. of *New Poems 1954*, ed. Rex Warner, Christopher Massal and Laurie Lee. *Swatantra*, 11 June 1955:30-31.
Rev. of *Wedding Preparations in the Country and Other Posthumous Prose Writings* by Franz Kafka. *Swatantra*, 9 July 1955: 32-35.
Rev. of *The Collected Poems of Wallace Stevens*. *Swatantra*, 23 July 1955:33-36.
Rev. of *Sex, Literature and Censorship* by D.H. Lawrence. *Swatantra*, 30 July 1955:35+.
Rev. of *My Many Coated-Man* by Laurie Lee. *Swatantra*, 13 Aug. 1955:36-37.
Rev. of *Jumping Joan and Other Stories* by C.M.B. Kitchin. *Swatantra*, 10 Sept. 1955:35+.
Rev. of *A Rose for Winter* by Laurie Lee. 24 Sept. 1955:35-36.
Rev. of *Stories from Indian Classics* by V.S. Naravane. ts.

Secondary Sources

Allen, Walter. *The Short Story in English*. Oxford: Clarendon Press, 1981.
Aldridge, John W., ed. *Critics and Essays on Modern Fiction*. New York: Arnold, 1952.
Altenbernd, Lynn and Leslie L. Lewis. *A Handbook for the Study of Fiction*. London: Macmillan, 1966.
Anand, Mulk Raj. *The Lost Child and Other Stories*. London: J.A. Allen, 1934.
______. *Untouchable* 1935. New Delhi: Arnold Heinemann, 1936.
______. *Lament on the Death of a Master of Arts*. Lucknow: Naya Sansar, 1939.
______. *Across the Blackwaters*. London: Jonathan Cape, 1940.
______. *The Sword and the Sickle*. London: Jonathan Cape, 1942.
______. *The Barber's Trade Union and Other Stories*. London: Jonathan Cape, 1944.
______. *The Power of Darkness and Other Stories*. Bombay: Jaico, 1959.
______. *Lajwanti and Other Stories*. Bombay: Jaico, 1969.
______. *Between Tears and Laughter*. New Delhi: Sterling, 1973.
______. *Seven Summers*. New Delhi: Arnold Heinemann India, 1987.
Anderson, Sherwood. *Ten Modern Masters: An Anthology of the Short Story*. New York: Harcourt, Brace and World, 1953.
Anjaneyulu, D. "The Stories of Manjeri S. Isvaran." *Thought*, 10 Aug. 1956:12-13.
Apter, T.E. *Fantasy Literature: An Approach to Reality*. Bloomington: Indiana UP, 1982.
Ayyer, A.S.P. *Indian After-Dinner Stories*. Madras: Teachers, 1929.
Baldeshwiler, Eileen. "The Lyric Short Story: The Sketch of a History." *Studies in Short Fiction*. Summer 1969:443-53.
Bates, H.E. *The Modern Short Story from 1809 to 1953*. London: Robert Hale, 1988.
Bhatnagar, M.K. *Political Consciousness in Indian English Writing*. New Delhi: Bahri, 1991.
Biswal, Jayant K. *A Critical Study of the Novels of R.K. Narayan*. New Delhi: Nirmal, 1987.

Bonheim, Helmut. *The Narrative Modes: Techniques of the Short Story*. 1982. Cambridge: D.S. Brewer, 1986.

Bose, Sunil Kumar. Rev. of *Rickshawallah* by Isvaran. *Modern Review*, 6 Sept. 1947:40.

Brooks, Cleanth and Robert Penn Warren. *The Scope of Fiction*. New York: Appleton Crafts Division of Meredith Corporation, 1960.

Brown, Calvin S., ed. *The Reader's Companian to World Literature*. New York: New American Library, n.d.

Brown, Suzanne Hunder, "'Tess' and 'Tess': An Experiment in Genre." *Modern Fiction Studies, Modern Short Story*. Spring 1982:38-41.

Burnley, Judith, ed. *Penguin Modern Stories 4*. Middlesex: Penguin, 1970.

Chakravarti, Khetrapal. *Sarada and Hingena*. Calcutta: Basu Mitra, 1986.

Chandrasekharan, K. "Manjeri Isvaran's Stories." *The Hindu*, 29 Jan. 1956:n.p.

Chekhov, Anton. *Plays and Stories*. Trans. S.S. Koteliansky. London: Everyman's Library, 1941.

CIEFL. *A Bibliography of Indian English*. Hyderabad: CIEFL, 1972.

Coates, Irene. Rev. of *Rhapsody in Red* by Manjeri S. Isvaran. *Swatantra*, July 1956:33+.

Cornelia, Sorabji. *Love and Life behind the Purdah*. London: 1901.

Dastoor, P.E. "Manjeri Isvaran's Short Stories." *Sunday*, 15 July 1956.

Davis, Robert Gorham, ed. *Ten Modern Masters: An Anthology of the Short Story*. New York: Harcourt, Brace and World, 1953.

Dey, Esha. *The Novels of Raja Rao*. New Delhi: Prestige, 1992.

Dhawan, R.K. *Explorations in Modern Indo-English Fiction*. New Delhi: Bahri, 1992.

Dietrich, R.F. and Roger M. Sundell. Introduction. *The Art of Fiction*. New York: Holt, Rinehart and Winston, 1978.

Dutt, Shosheee Chunder. *The Times of Yore: Tales from Indian History*. London: Lovell Reeve, 1985.

Eliot, T.S. "Tradition and the Individual Talent." *English Critical Texas*, ed. D.J. Enright and Ernest De Chickera. London: Oxford UP, 1964:293-301.

Gaer, Joseph. *The Fables of India*. Boston: Little Brown, 1955.

Gardner, John and Lennis Dunlap. *The Forms of Fiction*. New York: Random House, 1962.

Gupta, G.S. Balarama. *Essays on Indian Writing in English*. Gulbarga: JIWE, 1975.

______.. *Mulk Raj Anand*. Bareilly: Prakash, 1974.

Hall, James B. and Joseph Hand, ed. *The Short Story*. New York: Macmillan, 1956.

Hale, Nancy. *The Realities of Fiction: An Author Talks about Writing*. London: Macmillan, 1963.

Hampson, John. Introduction. *No Ankletbells for Her* by Isvaran. Madras: Mitra, 1949, vii-xvi.

Handford, S.A., ed. *Critics and Essays on Modern Fiction*. New York: Arnold, 1952.

Hanson, Clare and Andrew Curr. *Katherine Mansfield*. London: Macmillan, 1981.

Hardy, Barbara. *The Advantages of Lyric: Essays on Feeling in Poetry*. Bloomington: Indiana UP, 1977.

Hookens, William. "The Long Short Story in India." *Thought*, 26 Oct. 1951:12-13.

Hormasji, Nariman. *Katherine Mansfield: An Appraisal*. London: Collins, 1967.

Hudson, Derek, ed. *Modern English Short Stories*. 1956. London: Oxford UP, 1963.

Jain, Sushil Kumar. *A Select Bibliography of Indian Short Stories*. Vol. XII, No. 2, 1969.

Karkala, John A. and Leena. *A Select Bibliography of Indo-English Literature*. Bombay: Nirmala Sadanand, 1974.

Kesavan, R.S. and V.Y. Kulkarni, ed. "The National Bibliography of Indian Literature." 1901-1953, Vol. 1. New Delhi: Sahitya Akademi, 1962.

Liddel, Robert. *Some Principles of Fiction*. London: Jonathan Cape, 1963.

Iyengar, K.R. Srinivasa. Rev. of *Painted Tigers* by Isvaran. *The Aryan Path*, Nov. 1956:521.

______. *Indian Writing in English*. New Delhi: Sterling, 1984.
Jackson, Rose Mary. *Fantasy: The Literature of Subversion*. London: Methuen, 1981.
Jha, Rama. *Gandhian Thought and Indo-Anglian Novelists*. Delhi: Chanakya, 1983.
Johns, Phyllis M., ed. *Modern English Short Stories*. 1939. London: Oxford UP, 1963.
Kaushik, Asha. *Politics, Aesthetics and Culture: A Study of Indo-Anglian Political Novel*. New Delhi: Manohar, 1988.
Kempton, Kenneth Payson. *The Short Story*. Cambridge: Harvard UP, 1954.
Kennedy, X.J. *An Introduction to Fiction*. Boston: Little, Brown, 1987.
Kirpal, Viney, ed. *The New Indian Novel in English*. Bombay: Allied, 1990.
Kripalani, Krishna. *Modern Indian Literature*. Bombay: Nirmala Sadanand, 1968.
Krishnan, S., ed. *Malgudi Landscapes: The Best of R.K. Narayan*. New Delhi: Penguin, 1992.
Kumar, Shiv K., ed, *Modern Indian Short Stories*. Delhi: Oxford UP, 1983.
Lohafer, Susan. *Coming to Terms with the Short Story*. Baton Rouge: Louisiana State UP, 1983.
Longfellow, Henry Wordsworth. *Hawthorne and the Critical Heritage*. London: Routledge and Kegan Paul, 1970.
Lubbock, Percy. *The Craft of Fiction*. London: Jonathan Cape, 1965.
Madhaviah, A. *Kusika's Short Stories*. Madras: The Author's Press, 1924.
Madhaviah, P. "Book Reviews." *Sunday Times*, 2 Feb. 1958.
Mansfield, Katherine. *In a German Pension*. London: Stephen Swift, 1911.
______., *The Complete Stories of Katherine Mansfield*. Auckland: Golden Press, 1978.
Matlaw, Myron and Leonard Lief. *Story and Critic*. New York: Harper and Row, 1963.
Maugham, W. Somerset. *Selected Prefaces and Introductions of Somerset Maughan*. London: Heinemann, 1963.
______. *Points of View*. London: Heinemann, 1958.
Mehta, P.P. *Indo-Anglian Fiction: An Assessment*. Bareilly: Prakash, 1968.
Merson, A.O., ed. *Modern Short Stories*. London: Macmillan, 1963.
Miller Jr., James E. and Bernice Slot, ed. *The Dimensions of Short Story: A Critical Anthology*. New York: Dodd, Mead, 1972.
Mizener, Arthur, ed. *Short Stories: Use of Imagination*. New York: W.W. Norton, 1967.
MKR. Rev. of *Painted Tigers* by Isvaran. *Indian Express*, 8 Jan. 1956:n.p.
Mukherjee Meenakshi. *The Twice Born Fiction*. 1971. New Delhi: Arnold Heinemann, 1974.
Murti, K.V. Suryanarayana. *Kohinoor in the Crown: Critical Studies in Indian English Literature*. New Delhi: Sterling, 1987.
Naik, M.K. *Mirror on the Wall: Images of India and the Englishman in Anglo-Indian Fiction*. New Delhi: Sterling, 1991.
______. ed. *Perspectives on Indian Fiction in Engligh*. New Delhi: Abhinav, 1985.
______. *Indian English Short Story: A Representative Anthology*. New Delhi: Arnold Heinemann, 1984.
______. *A History of Indian English Literature*. New Delhi: Sahitya Akademi, 1982.
______, S.K. Desai and G.S. Amur, ed. *Critical Essays on Indian Writing in English*. Dharwar: Karnataka University, 1968.
Narasimhaiah, C.D. *Raja Rao*. New Delhi: Arnold Heinemann, India, n.d.
______., ed. *Fiction and the Reading Public in India*. Mysore: University of Mysore, 1967.
Narasimhan, Raji. "Tamil Imagery, English Idiom." *The Sunday Standard*, 16 June 1963:n.p.
Narayan, R.K. *Dodu and Other Stories*. Mysore: Indian Thought Publications, 1943.
______.. *The English Teacher*. Mysore: Indian Thought Publications, 1963.
______.. *An Astrologer's Day and Other Stories*. 1947. Mysore: Indian Thought Publications, 1964.

______.. *A Horse and Two Goats.* Mysore: Indian Thought Publications, 1970.
______.. *Malgudi Days.* Madras: Allied, 1982.
______.. *Under the Banyan Tree and Other Stories.* London: Heinemann, 1985.
______. *Cyclone and Other Stories.* Mysore: Indian Thought Publications, n.d.
Narayan, Syamala A. *Raja Rao: Man and His Works.* New Delhi: Sterling, 1988.
Nehru, Jawaharlal. *An Autobiography.* 1936. New Delhi: Oxford UP, 1986.
Neogi, Dwijendra Nath. *Sacred Tales of India.* London: Macmillan, 1916.
Niven, Alastair. *The Yoke of Pity: A Study in the Fictional Writings of Mulk Raj Anand.* New Delhi: Arnold Heinemann, 1978.
O'Connor, Frank. *The Lonely Voice: A Study of the Short Story.* London: Methuen, 1963.
______. ed. *Modern Irish Short Stories.* London: Oxford UP, 1957.
O'Connor, William Van. *Forms of Modern Fiction.* Bloomington: Indiana UP, 1948.
O'Faolin, Sean. *The Short Story.* London: Collins, 1948.
Palgrave. Preface. *Golden Treasury of Songs and Lyrics.* Ed. J.M. Fowler. London: Macmillan, 1959, vii-ix.
Paniker, K. Ayyappa et al. *Kerala Writers in English.* 5. series 1. Madras: Macmillan India, 1983.
Pawate, C.I. *The Panchantantra and Aesop's Fables.* Delhi: Amar, 1986.
Perrine, Laurence. *Story and Structure.* New York: Harcourt, Brace and World, 1969.
Philip, David Scott. *Perceiving India through the Works of Nirad C. Chaudhuri, R.K. Narayan and Ved Mehta.* New Delhi: Sterling, 1986.
Prasad, Madhusudan, ed. *Contemporary Indian English Stories.* New Delhi: Sterling, 1983.
Prescott, Peter S., ed. *The Norton Book of American Short Stories.* New York: W.W. Norton, 1988.
Radhakrishnan, N. *Indo-Anglian Fiction: Major Trends and Themes.* Madras: Emerald, 1984.
Rajan P.K. *Studies in Mulk Raj Anand.* New Delhi: Abhinav, 1986.
______. *The Growth of the Novel in India.* New Delhi: Abhinav, 1989.
Ram, Atma. *Perspectives on R.K. Narayan.* Ghaziabad: Vimal, 1981.
Rao, Raja. *The Cow of the Barricades and Other Stories.* Madras: Oxford UP, 1947.
______. *The Policeman and the Rose.* Delhi: Oxford UP, 1978.
______. *Kanthapura.* New Delhi: Oxford UP, 1989.
Rao, M. Rama, ed. *Fiction and Reading Public in India.* Mysore: U of Mysore, 1967.
Reddy, Obula P. "The Short Stories of Katherine Mansfied: A Study in Themes and Techniques." Diss., Sri Krishnadevaraya U, 1987.
Reddy, K. Venkata. *The Major Indian Novelists.* New Delhi: Prestige, 1990.
______.. "An Adolescent Encounter with Death: Katherine Mansfield's 'The Garden Party.'" *Kakatiya Journal of English Studies,* ix (1988-89):1-10, n.p.
Reid, Ian. *The Short Story.* London: Methuen, n.d.
Rodway, Allan. *The Truths of Fiction.* London: Chatto and Windus, 1970.
Rohrberger, Mary. *Hawthorne and the Modern Short Story: A Study in Genre.* The Hague: Mouton, 1966.
Sarma, G.P. *Nationalism in Indo-Anglian Fiction.* 1978. New Delhi: Sterling, 1990.
Saxena, O.P. *Glimpses of Indo-English Fiction.* New Delhi: Jainsons, 1985.
Saxena, Man Mohan, ed. *Indian Short Stories.* Calcutta: Oxford UP, 1950.
Sen, Dileepkumar, ed. *Indian Short Stories.* Calcutta: Oxford UP, 1950.
Sharma, K.K., ed. *Perspectives on Mulk Raj Anand.* Ghaziabad: Vimal, 1978.
Sharrad, Paul. *Raja Rao and Cultural Tradition.* Delhi: Sterling, 1987.
Shaw, Harry and Douglas Beiment. *Reading the Short Story.* New York: Harper, 1941.
Shaw, Valerie. *The Short Story: A Critical Introduction.* London: Longman, 1983.
Short, Raymond W. and Richard B. Sewall, ed. *Short Story for Study: An Anthology.* New York: Henry Holt, 1941.

"Sidelights." *Swatantra*, 14 Feb. 1953:40+.
Singh, Avadhesh K. *Contemporary Indian Fiction in English*. New Delhi: Creative, 1993.
Singh, Karan. *Prophet of Indian Nationalism*. Bombay: Bharatiya Vidya Bhavan, 1967.
Sinha, U.P. *Patterns of Myth and Reality: A Study in R.K. Narayan's Novels*. Delhi: Sandarbh, 1988.
Smith, A.J. and W.H. Mason, ed. *Short Story Study: A Critical Anthology*. London: Edward Arnold, 1961.
Sorabji, Cornelia. *Indian Tales of Great Ones*. London: Blackie, 1916.
Stewart, Randall and Dorothy Bethrum, ed. *Classic American Fiction*, US: Scott Foresman, 1954.
Stone, Wilfred, Nancy Huddleton Packer, Robert Hoopes, ed. *The Short Story: An Introduction*. New York: McGraw Hill, 1976.
Subramanyam, KA NA. "English Poetry Written in India." *The Sunday Standard*, 23 Oct. 1966:n.p.
Tagore, Rabindranath. *Hungry Stones and Other Stories*. London: Macmillan, 1950.
Tandon, P.D. Rev. of *Naked Shingles* by Isvaran. *The National Herald*, 9 March 1942:n.p.
The Pancha Tantra. Trans. Arthur Ryder. Bomaby: Jaico, 1975.
Townsend, Rochelle S., trans. and ed. *Russian Short Stories*. London: J.M. Dent, 1861.
Venkataramni, K.S. *Kandan the Patriot*. Madras: Swetaranya·Ashrama, 1934.
______., *Murugan the Tiller*. Madras: Swetaranya Ashrama, 1929.
______., *Jatadharan and Other Stories*. Madras: Swetaranya Ashrama, 1937.
______., "Manjeri S. Isvaran." ts. Personal Library of Isvaran, New Delhi.
Venkateswaran, Shyamala. *Indian Fiction in English: A Bibliography*. Mysore: U of Mysore, 1970.
V.M.I. Rev. of *Angry Dust* by Isvaran. *The Aryan Path*, May 1944:233+.
Venugopal, C.V. *The Indian Short Story in English*. Bareilly: Prakash, n.d.
Verghese C. Paul. *Problems of the Indian Creative Writer in English*. Bombay: Somaiya, 1971.
Vighneswara. "Sotto Voice: Diverse in Strange Seas." *Swatantra*, 7 Sept. 1959:3+.
Walsh, William. *Indian Literature in English*. London: Longman, 1990.
______., ed. *Readings in Commonwealth Literature*. Oxford: Clarendon Press, 1973.
Warfel, Harry R. and G. Harrison Orians, ed. *American Local Colour Stories*. New York: American Book Company, 1941.
Welty, Eudora. "The Reading and Writing of Short Story." *Atlantic Monthly*, February 1949.
West, Muriel. "Finished Workman." ts. Personal Library of Isvaran, New Delhi.
West, Roy B. Jr. and Robert Wooster Stallman. *The Art of Modern Fiction*. New York: Rinehart, 1949.
Williams, Haydn Moore. *Galaxy of Indian Writings in English*. Delhi: Akshat, New Delhi.

Index